I0821110

NASCAR®

RACE DAY EATS

TAILGATE PARTY RECIPES

REDDICK
CAMRY
TRUEX JR.
GIBBS
BUSCH
LAJOIE
GAINBRIDGE
GILLILAND
HEMRIC
LARSON
BLANEY
WABASH
PREECE
CINDRIC
ELLIOTT
NAPA
SUÁREZ
CHASTAIN
BERRY
KESELOWSKI
EDGE
MCDOWELL
Delo
Love's

NASCAR RACE DAY EATS

TAILGATE PARTY RECIPES

Recipes and photography by **Mike Lang**
With additional text by **Kelly Crandall**
Foreword by **Joey Logano**

INSIGHT EDITIONS
SAN RAFAEL • LOS ANGELES • LONDON

CONTENTS

2023
CHAMPION
RYAN BLANEY
2023
NASCAR CUP SERIES
PHOENIX RACEWAY
PHOENIX RACEWAY

START YOUR ENGINES!

It's long been said, but there are few things that come close to the experience of a NASCAR race in person. From the sensory overload of the roar of the engines to following on-track battles between the best drivers in the world, NASCAR's storied, seventy-five-plus-year history only continues to transcend into new generations and destinations across the world.

All this isn't possible without the most passionate fans in all of sports. NASCAR fans may never agree on which drivers are worthy of cheers or boos each week—trust me, I may know this better than anyone—but where they do find common ground is in the campground. No race weekend is complete without a top-tier tailgate setup in the infield; it's what makes our sport so unique. Where else can you spend the weekend camping inside the stadium of where your favorite team is playing?

Whether you're driving around a packed infield ahead of the Daytona 500 or following the crowds down Talladega Boulevard, there's a whole other side of the sensory overload you'll experience at the track. From the grills firing up barbecue in Kansas City to the traditional Labor Day weekend cookouts at Darlington—even extending as far as the garage area where my wife's world-famous salsa and dips are gone within minutes of setting them down in the hauler—NASCAR's tailgating scene has it all.

Now it's time for you to bring these race day recipes to your tailgate.

—Joey Logano

Three-Time NASCAR Cup Series Champion

DIPS

ALEXBOWMAN
CHEVROLET
AXALTA
MAC TOOLS
SIEMENS
NASCAR
CUP SERIES
EAGLE
GOODYEAR

SOUTHWEST CORN DIP

DIFFICULTY: Rookie | **PREP TIME:** 4 minutes | **SERVES:** 8 | **DIETARY:** GF, V

THIS SOUTHWEST CORN DIP is perfect for a southwest NASCAR race. It's super cool, bold, and zesty, like a day at Texas Motor Speedway in Fort Worth, Texas, or Phoenix Raceway in Avondale, Arizona. Though these facilities are different sizes, with Texas at 1.5 miles and Phoenix Raceway at 1 mile, they prove equally fun environments for race fans. It'll take no time to whip up this dip for you and your friends to enjoy. Scoop with chips or pile onto tacos and nachos!

1 can (15 ounces) whole corn kernels, drained

1 cup mayonnaise

1 cup sour cream

½ cup cotija cheese, finely grated

1 tablespoon canned chipotles in adobo sauce, puréed

2 teaspoons finely chopped fresh chives

2 teaspoons freshly squeezed lime juice

1 teaspoon cumin powder

½ teaspoon garlic powder

¼ teaspoon kosher salt

1. In a medium bowl, combine the ingredients and serve.
2. For best results, cover and refrigerate for at least 1 hour before serving.

FUN FACT

NASCAR stands for the National Association for Stock Car Auto Racing. It was established in December 1947 by Bill France Sr. during a meeting at the Streamline Hotel in Daytona Beach, Florida. Known as the "Birthplace of NASCAR," the Streamline Hotel remains operational and is a popular tourist destination.

CHIPOTLE RANCH DIP

DIFFICULTY: Rookie | **PREP TIME:** 4 minutes | **SERVES:** 8 | **DIETARY:** GF, V

WHEN YOU NEED SOMETHING easy and tasty for your race day gathering, blending together a Chipotle Ranch Dip is a winning decision. This dish combines the smooth taste you expect from a dip, plus a smoky, spicy kick from the chipotle pepper powder. So pull up a chair, grab your snacks, and be ready to fight off your friends because you'll want this creamy dip all to yourself!

1 cup mayonnaise

1 cup sour cream

1 tablespoon plus 1 teaspoon freshly squeezed lemon juice

2 teaspoons dried parsley

2 teaspoons dried dill

2 teaspoons dried chives

1 teaspoon dried chipotle pepper powder

½ teaspoon onion powder

½ teaspoon garlic powder

¼ teaspoon kosher salt

1. In a medium bowl, combine all the ingredients.
2. For best results, refrigerate for at least 1 hour prior to serving.

GRILLED SALSA

DIFFICULTY: Veteran | **PREP TIME:** 5 minutes | **COOK TIME:** 16 minutes | **SERVES:** 8 | **DIETARY:** GF, V

BE THE CREW CHIEF of your tailgate by choosing what goes on your baked potato with a fully loaded, flavor-packed baked potato bar! Whether you're heaping on sour cream or cheddar cheese, the choices are endless, so enjoy crafting your potato just the way you want it, like customizing a race car. With so many winning toppings, this baked potato bar is a champion!

1 pound Roma tomatoes, halved

1 poblano pepper, halved, ribs and seeds removed

1 serrano pepper, halved, ribs and seeds removed

1 large sweet onion, quartered

1 teaspoon olive oil

1 garlic clove

¼ cup fresh cilantro leaves

Juice of 1 lime

Kosher salt

EQUIPMENT

Perforated grill pan

1. In a large bowl, combine the tomatoes, poblano, serrano, and onion. Toss with the olive oil.
2. Prepare the grill for direct, medium-high heat cooking (400° to 450° F). Preheat the grill pan.
3. Put the vegetables on the grill pan and cook until soft and blistered, 10 to 12 minutes, flipping once. Remove the tomatoes and peppers. Continue to cook the onions until tender, 2 to 4 minutes more. Remove the onions. If desired, remove the tomato skins and discard.
4. Put the cooked vegetables in a food processor or blender. Add the garlic, cilantro, and lime. Pulse to the desired consistency. Add salt to taste.
5. Pour into a bowl and serve.

THE SOUTHERN 500 PIMENTO CHEESE

DIFFICULTY: Rookie | **PREP TIME:** 5 minutes | **COOK TIME:** 8 minutes | **SERVES:** 6 | **DIETARY:** GF

PIMENTO CHEESE, A SOUTHERN classic, is as tough as Darlington Raceway, a 1.366-mile track that can also be described as a Southern classic. But there's nothing tough about making this sharp, cheesy dip! With minimal prep and cook time, your taste buds will relish this creamy, smoky, and tangy combo. The bold cheese and crispy bacon contrast nicely with the smooth, velvety base of the cream cheese, mayo, and sour cream. Use this dip on whatever you wish!

4 slices bacon

8 ounces cream cheese, softened

2 cups shredded cheddar cheese

¼ cup mayonnaise

¼ cup sour cream

One 4-ounce jar pimentos, drained

¼ teaspoon onion powder

¼ teaspoon garlic powder

¼ teaspoon cayenne pepper

¼ teaspoon black pepper

1. In a large skillet, cook the bacon over medium heat to your desired level of doneness, flipping once, 6 to 8 minutes.
2. Remove the bacon from the skillet and coarsely chop.
3. Put the bacon, along with the rest of the ingredients, in a medium bowl and combine.
4. Serve with crackers or chips.

FUN FACT

The Southern 500, held at Darlington Raceway, is among the most prestigious and storied races on the NASCAR calendar. It was run for the first time in 1950, won by Johnny Mantz, and at 500 miles, it was one of the longest races on the schedule. The track has many nicknames, most notably being "Too Tough to Tame" for its grueling toll on drivers who have to run inches from the wall.

STARTERS

MAC & CHEESE BITES

DIFFICULTY: Veteran | **PREP TIME:** 6 Minutes | **COOK TIME:** 45 Minutes | **SERVINGS:** 8

RACE FANS, BRING YOUR appetites! These gooey Mac & Cheese Bites are a hit with drivers throughout the garage area—and they'll be a hit with you too when you include them at your tailgate! Who doesn't love a fun twist on a lifelong cheesy favorite? Drivers can grab these crispy, mildly spicy snacks on the go during pre-race activities like meetings, fan appearances, and driver introductions. And you can enjoy these crunchy, bite-size snacks sitting with friends!

½ pounds macaroni elbows

2 tablespoons unsalted butter

2 tablespoons all-purpose flour

1½ cups whole milk

4 cups shredded cheddar cheese

2 teaspoons ground mustard

½ teaspoon kosher salt

1 teaspoon hot sauce

1 jalapeño, seeds and ribs removed, diced

¼ cup panko breadcrumbs

Nonstick spray

EQUIPMENT

Mini muffin pan

Hickory smoking wood chunks or chips

1. Bring a large pot of water to a boil. Cook the macaroni to al dente, about 6 minutes. Drain and set aside.
2. In a large skillet, melt the butter over medium heat. Whisk in the flour. Increase the heat to medium-high and whisk in the milk. Cook, stirring constantly, until the sauce thickens, 4 to 5 minutes.
3. Reduce the heat to medium-low and stir in the cheese. Once melted, stir in the mustard, salt, hot sauce, and jalapeños.
4. In a large bowl, combine the cheese sauce and cooked macaroni.
5. Spray the muffin pan with the nonstick spray.
6. Fill the muffin pan cups with macaroni and cheese. Top with the panko breadcrumbs.
7. Prepare the grill for indirect, medium-high heat cooking (400° to 450° F).
8. If using a charcoal grill, add three or four wood chunks directly to the lit coals once the coals have ashed over. If using a gas grill, add the wood chunks to a pouch made of aluminum foil with holes poked through the top. Put the pouch directly over a lit burner. Once the gas or charcoal grill begins to release white, wispy smoke, it's ready.
9. Grill the pan over indirect medium-high heat until the cheese begins to brown, 35 to 40 minutes.
10. Remove from the grill and allow to cool for 10 minutes. Remove and serve.

POLE POSITION PORK BUTT BURNT ENDS

DIFFICULTY: Veteran | **PREP TIME:** 20 Minutes | **COOK TIME:** 5 Hours | **SERVINGS:** 10

THE FASTEST DRIVER FROM qualifying that takes place early in race weekends earns the reward to start Sunday race day from the "pole position," which is in first place. One of the tastiest tailgates starts with Pole Position Pork Butt Burnt Ends, which is a mouthwateringly delicious BBQ delicacy. Don't miss a chance to get your party going by smoking the meat for nearly as long as the race itself for a caramelized, earthy smokiness that's equal parts sweet and savory—and sticky, too!

1 boneless pork butt (6 to 8 pounds)

RUB

¼ cup paprika

¼ cup dark brown sugar

2 tablespoons ground cumin

1 tablespoon garlic powder

1 tablespoon onion powder

1 tablespoon kosher salt

1 tablespoon black pepper

1 cup BBQ sauce

⅓ cup unsalted butter

½ cup brown sugar

EQUIPMENT

Hickory smoking chunks or chips

Large foil pan

1. Remove any hard fat from the pork shoulder and then cut the pork into roughly 1½-by-2-inch pieces.
2. In a small bowl, combine the rub ingredients.
3. Generously cover the pork all over with the rub. Tip: Because the pork pieces are small, it's helpful to place them on a wire rack to move them on and off the grill.
4. Prepare the grill for indirect, low heat cooking (250° to 300° F).
5. If using a charcoal grill, add three or four wood chunks directly to the lit coals once the coals have ashed over. If using a gas grill, add the wood chunks to a pouch made of aluminum foil with holes poked through the top. Put the pouch directly over a lit burner. Once the gas or charcoal grill begins to release white, wispy smoke, it's ready.
6. Cook the pork over indirect low heat until the internal temperature reads 165° F with an instant-read thermometer, 2½ to 3 hours.
7. Place the pork in a large disposable foil pan, top with the BBQ sauce, butter, and brown sugar, and cover tightly with aluminum foil.
8. Return the pork to the grill and continue to cook for 1 hour. Stir the pork halfway through to ensure the pieces are covered in sauce.
9. Remove the foil from the pan and continue to cook until the internal temperature of the pork reads 203° F with an instant-read thermometer, about 1 hour more.
10. Remove, allow to cool slightly, and serve.

BACON-WRAPPED SPICY TOTS

DIFFICULTY: Veteran | **PREP TIME:** 15 Minutes | **COOK TIME:** 1 Hour | **SERVINGS:** 6

THE FIRST NASCAR ALL-STAR Race at Charlotte Motor Speedway in 1992 was dubbed "One Hot Night" and lived up to the hype with Davey Allison crossing first across the finish line after a hard-fought battle in the final laps. Add an irresistibly juicy burst of flavor in your tailgate with these tots that explode with the crispy, saltiness of bacon and the hot, fiery kick of cayenne.

¼ cup brown sugar

¼ teaspoon cayenne pepper

2 cups frozen tater tots (about 30 tots)

10 slices bacon

¼ cup mayonnaise

¼ cup sour cream

1 tablespoon sriracha

1. Prepare the grill for indirect, low heat cooking (250° to 300° F).
2. In a small bowl, combine the brown sugar and cayenne pepper.
3. Coat the tater tots in the sugar mixture.
4. Cut each slice of bacon into three equal pieces.
5. Wrap each tater tot with a piece of bacon and place seam down on a tray.
6. Grill the bacon-wrapped tots over indirect heat, with the seam down, until the bacon has crisped to your liking and the tater tot cooked through, about 1 hour.
7. In a small bowl, combine the mayonnaise, sour cream, and sriracha. Serve with the bacon-wrapped tots.

FUN FACT

The 1992 All-Star Race was also the first NASCAR event held at an intermediate racetrack at night, since it utilized artificial lighting. Today, several races on the NASCAR schedule take place at night, including those at Charlotte Motor Speedway.

JALAPEÑO POPPERS

DIFFICULTY: Veteran | **PREP TIME:** 20 Minutes | **COOK TIME:** 1 Hour | **SERVINGS:** 8 | **DIETARY:** GF

WHAT NASCAR FAN DOESN'T love these fiery Jalapeño Poppers?! If it's not the spice that kicks your taste buds into high gear, it's the crunchy, creamy filling. These high-octane, cheesy bites race ahead of the competition with rich, savory pork sausage and spicy pepper jack cheese.

½ pound pork sausage

8 jalapeños

8 ounces cream cheese, room temperature

2 teaspoon BBQ rub (page 24), divided

½ cup shredded pepper jack cheese

Parmesan cheese, grated, for topping

EQUIPMENT

Hickory smoking chunks or chips

1. Prepare the grill for indirect, low heat cooking (250° to 300° F).
2. If using a charcoal grill, add three or four wood chunks directly to the lit coals once the coals have ashed over. If using a gas grill, add the wood chunks to a pouch made of aluminum foil with holes poked through the top. Put the pouch directly over a lit burner. Once the gas or charcoal grill begins to release white, wispy smoke, it's ready.
3. In a small skillet, cook the pork over medium heat until browned and cooked through, 4 to 5 minutes. Set aside.
4. Cut each jalapeño in half lengthwise. Remove the seeds and ribs.
5. In a small bowl, combine the pork sausage, cream cheese, 1 teaspoon of BBQ rub, and the pepper jack cheese.
6. Fill each jalapeño with the cheese mixture. Top each jalapeño with the remaining 1 teaspoon of BBQ rub and the grated Parmesan cheese.
7. Cook the poppers over indirect low heat until cooked through, about 1 hour.

8. Remove and serve.

GRIDDLED NACHOS

DIFFICULTY: Rookie | **PREP TIME:** 8 Minutes | **COOK TIME:** 20 Minutes | **SERVINGS:** 12

GET REVVED UP FOR race day with a fun way to make a fan favorite. Grilling is a staple at tailgates, and NASCAR races are no different. Whether at Bristol or Atlanta, you'll find yourself the grill crew chief with these bold, smoky, and melty nachos. The ingredients are classics that make for a melt-in-your-mouth goodness. The preparation is easy—all you need are foil trays and a grill. This fast, cheesy dish is perfect when away from home but still wanting to eat like a champ.

1 pound tortillas chips

4 cups shredded cheddar cheese

One 15-ounce jar queso cheese

One 15-ounce can black beans, rinsed and drained

1 cup grape tomatoes, quartered

¼ cup ripe olives, sliced

4 green onions, green parts only, chopped

Pickled jalapeños, for topping

Sour cream, for topping

Fresh cilantro, chopped, for topping

OPTIONAL TOPPINGS

Pulled Pork (page 57)

BBQ Chicken (page 38)

EQUIPMENT

Two 9-by-13-inch aluminum foil trays

1. Make three layers of nachos in each foil tray. Start by spreading out a layer of chips topped with part of the cheddar cheese, queso, black beans, tomatoes, olives, and green onions. Repeat two more times.
2. Prepare the grill for indirect, medium heat cooking (350° to 400° F).
3. Grill the nachos over indirect medium heat until the nachos are heated through and the cheese has melted, 15 to 20 minutes.
4. Remove and top with the jalapeños, sour cream, and cilantro.
5. Serve warm.

FUN FACT

Denny Hamlin and Brad Keselowski are NASCAR drivers and owners. Hamlin drives for Joe Gibbs Racing, but owns the 23XI racing team with drivers Bubba Wallace, Tyler Reddick, and Riley Herbst. Keselowski drives for the team that he co-owns: RFK Racing.

GRILLED PIGS IN A BLANKET

DIFFICULTY: Veteran | **PREP TIME:** 25 Minutes | **COOK TIME:** 20 Minutes | **SERVINGS:** 10

FIRE UP THE GRILL! You'll be eating in style at your tailgate and will have others wanting to join your party when you put a spicy, smoky, cheesy twist on the classic pigs in a blanket. By adding the screaming flavor of blue cheese and jalapeño, this side dish is built for bold flavor and high-speed snacking, leaving you whooping and cheering about more than the action on the track!

1 sheet of puff pastry, thawed

1 jalapeño pepper, ribs and seeds removed, minced

5 ounces blue cheese, crumbled

30 cocktail franks

1 egg, beaten

BBQ sauce, for serving

1. Unfold a thawed sheet of puff pastry and cut ten 1-inch vertical columns. Then make two horizontal cuts to split each column into three equal pieces. Do not pull the pieces of puff pastry apart.
2. In a small bowl, combine the jalapeño and blue cheese.
3. Spread the cheese mixture across the puff pastry.
4. Place a cocktail frank on each piece of puff pastry and roll to create the blanket. Some stuffing will fall out, but stuff back as much as you can. Seal the end of the pastry with a brush of the beaten egg.
5. Prepare the grill for indirect, medium heat cooking (350° to 400° F).
6. Grill the pigs in a blanket over indirect medium heat until the cocktail frank is warmed through and the puff pastry is golden brown, 15 to 20 minutes.
7. Remove and serve with the BBQ sauce.

GRILLED CORN FRITTERS

DIFFICULTY: Veteran | **PREP TIME:** 5 Minutes | **COOK TIME:** 8 Minutes | **SERVINGS:** 4 | **DIETARY:** V

IOWA SPEEDWAY, IN NEWTON, Iowa, is surrounded by cornfields, and the winner of the NASCAR Cup Series race gets to take a big bite from an ear of corn in the victory lane. Ryan Blaney and the No. 12 Team Penske team were the first to experience the tradition after winning the inaugural Cup Series race at the track in 2024. These tasty Grilled Corn Fritters, with their smoky crunch and warm spice, will have your party guests racing back around for more than one bite.

Canola oil, for greasing

One 15-ounce can whole kernel corn, drained

¼ cup flour

1 teaspoon baking powder

1 teaspoon ancho chili powder

½ teaspoon salt

¼ teaspoon black pepper

1 egg

½ cup milk

2 green onions, chopped

Fresh cilantro, chopped

1. Prepare the griddle, or cast-iron skillet on the grill, for direct, medium-high heat cooking (400° to 450° F).
2. Place a thin coat of oil on the griddle and cook the corn until lightly charred, 3 to 4 minutes. Remove and set aside.
3. In a small bowl, combine the flour, salt, baking powder, ancho chili powder, and black pepper.
4. In a medium bowl, combine the egg and milk.
5. Whisk the dry ingredients into the wet ingredients. Once combined, stir in the corn and green onions.
6. Scoop ¼ cup of the batter and place on the griddle. Cook the fritters over medium-high heat until browned, 3 to 4 minutes, flipping once.
7. Remove, garnish with cilantro, and serve.

FUN FACT

Ryan Blaney is a second-generation NASCAR driver following in the footsteps of his father, Dave Blaney. Dave Blaney made 473 starts in the NASCAR Cup Series and concluded his career in 2004. Dave and Ryan were never able to compete against each other in the series.

MICHIGAN MEATBALLS

DIFFICULTY: Veteran | **PREP TIME:** 15 Minutes | **COOK TIME:** 10 Minutes | **SERVINGS:** 4

A PLACE MADE FOR speed, Michigan International Speedway is a favorite of Kevin Harvick, the 2014 Cup Series champion who is now retired, and Tyler Reddick. The two-mile oval allows drivers to use every inch of the track to rocket off the corners down the long straightaways. This meaty, powerhouse dish is perfect for a hearty race day treat.

MEATBALLS

1 pound 80/20 ground chuck

⅓ cup panko breadcrumbs

1 egg, beaten

¾ teaspoon kosher salt

½ teaspoon dried basil

¼ teaspoon onion powder

¼ teaspoon black pepper

SAUCE

¾ cup creamy peanut butter

¼ cup rice vinegar

¼ cup soy sauce

¼ cup honey

¼ teaspoon sesame oil

¼ teaspoon red pepper flakes

1 to 2 tablespoons water

1. In a medium bowl, combine the meatball ingredients using your hands. Be careful not to overwork the meat.
2. Make eight equal-size meatballs, each about 2 ounces.
3. In a small bowl, combine the peanut butter, vinegar, soy sauce, honey, sesame oil, and red pepper flakes. Add the water as needed to meet the desired consistency.
4. Prepare the grill for direct, medium heat cooking (350° to 400° F).
5. Grill the meatballs over direct medium heat until the internal temperature reads 155° F with an instant-read thermometer, 10 to 12 minutes, flipping once.
6. Remove and serve warm with the dipping sauce.

GRILLED FLATBREAD PIZZAS

DIFFICULTY: Rookie | **PREP TIME:** 8 Minutes | **COOK TIME:** 8 Minutes | **SERVINGS:** 4

DID YOU KNOW THAT certain racetracks in NASCAR are flat? New Hampshire Motor Speedway fits the bill for a flat track. And this dish fits the bill for flatbread—a Grilled Flatbread Pizza, that is! Although there are many pizza toppings to choose from, these delicious and healthy options are an excellent choice for your tailgate so that you can focus on getting ready to enjoy the race rather than having to spend much time preparing a meal. And yes, pineapple can go on pizza!

2 cups cooked chopped chicken*

1½ cups BBQ Sauce, divided

2 store-bought flatbreads

2 cups shredded mozzarella cheese

1 cup chopped pineapple (optional)

½ cup red onion, halved and sliced thinly

Fresh cilantro leaves, for topping

**For easy cooked chicken, shred a store-bought rotisserie chicken.*

1. In a medium bowl, combine the cooked chicken and 1 cup of BBQ sauce.
2. Evenly top the flatbread with the BBQ chicken, cheese, pineapple, and red onion.
3. Prepare the grill at medium-high heat for indirect cooking (400° to 450° F).
4. Grill the flatbread over indirect heat until the bread is crisp and the cheese is melted, 6 to 8 minutes.
5. Remove and top with cilantro and drizzle with the remaining BBQ sauce.

FUN FACT

The minimal banking at the one-mile track makes it seem even flatter when watching Joe Gibbs and racing drivers like Christopher Bell and Chase Briscoe roaring around the place!

ROTATION
FOR RACING PURPOSES
NOT FOR HIGHWAY USE

YELLOW FLAG HONEY CHIPOTLE WINGS

DIFFICULTY: Veteran | **PREP TIME:** 10 Minutes | **COOK TIME:** 55 Minutes | **SERVINGS:** 6 | **DIETARY:** GF

A TAILGATE IS THE perfect time to pull up a chair and gather with friends. But that means you need an easy-to-eat dish like finger foods. A yellow flag, otherwise known as a "caution flag" in a NASCAR race, plays the same role for drivers and teams by bringing the field back together and pausing the action when an incident needs attention. These sweet, smoky, and spicy wings are exactly what you need! They'll have you feeling full and ready to take on the rest of your day.

3 to 4 pounds chicken wings

1 teaspoon olive oil

1 teaspoon kosher salt

½ teaspoon black pepper

SAUCE

½ cup unsalted butter

⅓ cup chipotle peppers in adobo sauce, puréed

¼ cup honey

2 teaspoons apple cider vinegar

¼ teaspoon salt

1. With a pair of kitchen shears, prepare the chicken wings by cutting through the joints and separating the wing tip, flat, and drumette. Set the wing tips aside for another use.
2. Lightly brush the chicken with olive oil and season all over with salt and pepper.
3. Prepare the grill for indirect, low heat cooking (250° to 300° F).
4. Grill the chicken wings over indirect low heat until the internal temperature of the wing reads 165° F with an instant-read thermometer, about 45 minutes, flipping once.
5. Raise the grill temperature to indirect, medium-high heat cooking (450° to 500° F). Continue to grill the wings until the skin crispens, another 5 to 10 minutes.
6. To make the sauce, melt the butter in a small pan over medium-low heat. Stir in the remaining sauce ingredients. Reduce the heat to low and keep warm.
7. Remove the wings from the grill and toss with the sauce.
8. Serve warm.

SOUPS

DEWALT
20
yardnique
BELL
one can kill.

CINCINNATI-STYLE CHILI

DIFFICULTY: Rookie | **PREP TIME:** 10 Minutes | **COOK TIME:** 3 Hours | **SERVINGS:** 8

GET READY TO KICK back and enjoy race day after enjoying a hearty bowl of chili! Although Cincinnati isn't a hub for NASCAR, the city has a strong motorsports fanbase and is known for their delicious sweet and savory chili, which stands out for its unique, thin sauce and Mediterranean-inspired spices. Serve it over hot dogs or spaghetti—and enjoy!

4 cups water
2 pounds 90/10 ground beef
2 cups tomato sauce
One 12-ounce can tomato paste
1 yellow onion, grated
2 tablespoons chili powder
2 tablespoons active dry yeast
2 tablespoons sugar
1 tablespoon kosher salt
1 teaspoon ground cinnamon
1 teaspoon ground cumin
1 teaspoon garlic powder
½ teaspoon ground allspice
½ teaspoon ground black pepper
¼ teaspoon cayenne pepper
¼ teaspoon ground cloves
2 bay leaves

SERVE WITH

Shredded cheddar cheese
Cooked spaghetti
Chopped white onions
Hot dogs

1. In a large pot, combine all the ingredients* over medium-low heat for 3 hours, stirring occasionally.
2. Remove the bay leaves. Keep warm and serve.

***Note:** The ground beef is not browned prior to cooking and is added raw with the rest of the ingredients. This creates a more delicate and less beefy flavor synonymous with Cincinnati-Style Chili.

HAM & POTATO SOUP

DIFFICULTY: Veteran | **PREP TIME:** 10 Minutes | **COOK TIME:** 90 Minutes | **SERVINGS:** 4 | **DIETARY:** GF

THIS HAM AND POTATO soup is a true triumph, as far as soups go. Ham and potato go well together, like the best pairing of a crew chief and a driver in NASCAR. One of the most successful combinations in NASCAR was Jimmie Johnson and Chad Knaus, who won seven championships together at Hendrick Motorsports to tie legends Richard Petty and Dale Earnhardt. This creamy, savory soup is packed with flavor and goes full throttle on race day.

1 tablespoon olive oil

1 cup chopped yellow onion

½ cup chopped carrots

½ cup chopped celery

½ cups chopped cooked ham

4 cups chicken stock

2 pounds russet potatoes, peeled and chopped

1 cup heavy cream

½ teaspoon black pepper

Kosher salt

Green onion, chopped, for serving

1. In a large pot, warm the oil over medium heat. Add the onion, carrots, and celery and cook until translucent, 5 to 6 minutes.
2. Add the ham and cook for 2 minutes. Next, add the stock, bring to a boil, then cover and reduce the heat to a simmer, about 15 minutes.
3. Add the potatoes and cook until the potatoes are tender, about 1 hour.
4. Optional: Scoop half of the soup into a blender and pulse untill smooth. Return the soup to the pot. Doing so helps thicken the consistency.
5. Add the heavy cream and black pepper. Season to taste with salt.
6. Garnish with the green onion and serve warm.

FUN FACT

Jimmie Johnson and Chad Knaus were inducted into the NASCAR Hall of Fame together in 2024. Dale Earnhardt and Richard Petty were among those inducted in the inaugural NASCAR Hall of Fame Class of 2010.

HAMBURGER SOUP

DIFFICULTY: Rookie | **PREP TIME:** 8 Minutes | **COOK TIME:** 66 Minutes | **SERVINGS:** 8 | **DIETARY:** GF

THIS RACE DAY–READY, PERFECTLY tuned hamburger soup is an absolute go-to for NASCAR get-togethers, especially when inclement weather calls to stay inside and get comfortable by the TV. Make sure to invite fellow race fans over to enjoy a solid helping of ground beef, veggies, and potatoes with a side of Denny Hamlin domination in the No. 11 Joe Gibbs Racing car.

- 1 tablespoon olive oil
- 1 pound 80/20 ground chuck
- 4 cups beef broth
- 2 medium russet potatoes (about 2 cups), peeled and diced
- 2 cups frozen peas and carrots
- 2 cups tomato sauce
- 1 cup chopped onion
- ⅓ cup long grain rice
- 1 garlic clove, minced
- 1 teaspoon kosher salt
- ½ teaspoon black pepper

1. In a large pot, warm the olive oil over medium heat. Add the ground chuck and cook until browned, 5 to 6 minutes.
2. Add the remaining ingredients to the pot and bring to a boil, then reduce heat to low, cover, and simmer for 90 minutes.
3. Keep warm and serve.

KIDNEY BEAN SOUP

DIFFICULTY: Rookie | **PREP TIME:** 10 Minutes | **COOK TIME:** 90 Minutes | **SERVINGS:** 8 | **DIETARY:** GF

ENJOY THIS SIMPLE YET delicious soup on race day! Let the rich combination of beans and spices in a deep, savory broth bring as much comfort as the sight of race cars on the track. One of those places that brings such a warm, cozy feeling? The Indianapolis Motor Speedway. The Brickyard 400 is one of NASCAR's biggest races that every driver and team wants to win. It's an incredible sight to see a stock car going down the track's 3,300-foot frontstretch at full speed!

- One 15-ounce can dark kidney beans
- One 15-ounce can light kidney beans
- 3 cups russet potatoes, peeled and diced
- One 28-ounce can whole tomatoes
- 5 cups water, divided
- 1 tablespoon olive oil
- 1 cup yellow onion, diced
- 1 pound 90/10 ground beef
- 1 cup shredded cabbage
- ¼ cup chili powder
- 1 teaspoon kosher salt
- ½ teaspoon black pepper

1. In a large pot, combine the beans, potatoes, tomatoes, and 3 cups of water. Bring to a boil, cover, and then simmer for an hour over low heat.
2. Meanwhile, in a large skillet over medium heat, warm the olive oil. Once warmed, add the onion and cook until soft and translucent, 4 to 5 minutes. Next, add the ground beef and cook until browned, 6 to 7 minutes.
3. Add the meat mixture to the pot along with the cabbage and the remaining 2 cups of water. Stir until the chili powder, salt, and pepper. Bring to a boil, then reduce heat to low, and simmer for 30 minutes.
4. Keep warm and serve.

FUN FACT

There is a tradition at Indianapolis Motor Speedway for the winning driver and team: kissing the yard of bricks. The bricks are on the front stretch and serve as both the start and finish line. Dale Jarrett started the tradition of kissing the bricks after winning the Brickyard 400 in 1996.

BLACK FLAG BBQ CHICKEN SOUP

DIFFICULTY: Rookie | **PREP TIME:** 5 Minutes | **COOK TIME:** 45 Minutes | **SERVINGS:** 8

A BLACK FLAG IN NASCAR means a driver must leave the racetrack and head to pit road, the area found to the left of the racing surface where teams set up to work on the race cars. This flag can be issued for various reasons, such as a driver needing to pick up their speed or to address an issue with their race car. No matter the reason, the race has stopped, at least temporarily, for this driver. When you need to take some time for yourself, a nice soup is always the way to go. This bowl of BBQ chicken soup is easy to make and a full-throttle flavor ride for your taste buds.

2 pounds boneless, skinless chicken thighs

8 cups chicken stock

2 garlic cloves, minced

½ teaspoon ground cumin

½ teaspoon black pepper

2 cups store-bought BBQ sauce

2 cups frozen corn

One 15-ounce can Great Northern beans, drained and rinsed

Kosher salt

TOPPINGS

Sliced jalapeño

Fresh cilantro, chopped

Red onion, chopped

Shredded cheddar cheese

1. In a large pot, combine the chicken thighs, chicken stock, garlic, cumin, and pepper. Bring to a boil, then cover and reduce to a simmer until the internal temperature of the chicken reads 165° F with an instant-read thermometer, 14 to 16 minutes.
2. Remove the chicken from the pot and shred into pieces with two forks.
3. Return the chicken to the pot and add the BBQ sauce, corn, and beans. Bring to a boil and then reduce the heat and simmer for 30 minutes. Add salt to taste.
4. Serve warm with the toppings.

BREAKFAS

STS
LARSON

GREEN FLAG CINNAMON ROLL SANDWICHES

DIFFICULTY: Veteran | **PREP TIME:** 3 Minutes | **COOK TIME:** 20 Minutes | **SERVINGS:** 4

A TYPICAL DAY STARTS with breakfast, often referred to as the most important meal of the day. A NASCAR race begins with a green flag—one of the most important flags of the event! The green flag signifies the start of the race. It means step on the gas and go! So, start your day with this utterly indulgent breakfast. These champion-worthy sandwiches are a sweet twist on breakfast that will hit the spot while also tasting like a treat because of that warm, gooey icing.

Canola oil, for greasing

One 30-ounce bag frozen shredded hash browns

Kosher salt

4 maple sausage patties

4 eggs

One 12-ounce tube cinnamon rolls

4 slices colby cheese

EQUIPMENT

4 four-inch egg rings

Burger press

Basting dome or lid

1. Prepare the griddle or a cast-iron pan on the grill for direct, medium heat cooking (350° to 400° F).
2. Spread a thin layer of oil on the griddle. Place the egg rings on the griddle and fill each with shredded hash browns. Season lightly with salt.
3. Grill the hash browns until golden brown, 12 to 14 minutes, flipping once. Move to a cool part of the griddle.
4. While the hash browns are cooking, place the sausage patties on the griddle over direct medium heat and smash to roughly 4 inches in diameter with the burger press. Grill for 2 to 3 minutes, until cooked through, flipping once. Move to a cool part of the griddle.
5. Cook the eggs in the egg rings to your liking, depending on the style, 3 to 4 minutes.
6. Grill the cinnamon rolls over direct medium heat and smash to roughly 4 inches in diameter with the burger press. Grill until browned, 2 to 3 minutes, flipping once.
7. Make a sandwich by placing a griddled cinnamon roll on the griddle, followed by the hash brown, sausage patty, egg, and cheese. Add a small amount of water to the griddle by the sandwiches and cover with the basting dome to allow the cheese to melt, about 30 seconds. Top with the remaining grilled cinnamon roll and serve.

FUN FACT

The race begins with the field in a two-by-two formation. The drivers who qualified in an odd number starting position (i.e. third place, fifth place, and so on) are lined up on the inside row. The drivers who qualified in an even number starting position (i.e. fourth place, sixth place, and so on) are lined up on the outside row.

FUEL-ONLY BREAKFAST WRAPS

DIFFICULTY: Veteran | **PREP TIME:** 5 Minutes | **COOK TIME:** 25 Minutes | **SERVINGS:** 4

A QUICK AND EASY meal is often all that's needed to rev up your morning and start your race day off right. A little fuel to get things going is especially wonderful when there's no time to sit to dig into a full spread. A driver sometimes needs just a dash of fuel, usually as quick as 5 seconds, called a fuel-only pit stop, to get back into the race and make it to the finish. These wraps, with savory ground beef, creamy cheese, and fresh toppings, are a total game-changer.

Canola oil, for greasing
1 pound 90/10 ground beef
¼ cup taco seasoning
4 large eggs
1 teaspoon water
Five 12-inch flour tortillas
½ cup refried beans
½ cup nacho cheese
4 tostadas
½ cup sour cream
1⅓ cups bag shredded lettuce
1⅓ cups shredded cheddar cheese
1 Roma tomato, diced
¼ cup pickled jalapeños

1. Preheat the griddle for direct, medium heat cooking (350° to 400° F).
2. Apply a thin coat of oil to the surface of the griddle.
3. Add the ground beef to the griddle and top with the taco seasoning, working it in with a spatula. Cook the meat until browned, 8 to 9 minutes. Set aside.
4. In a small bowl, beat the eggs and water.
5. On the griddle over medium heat, cook the eggs until scramble, 3 to 4 minutes.
6. Cut one flour tortilla into quarters.
7. Place a whole tortilla on a clean work surface and top the center with 2 tablespoons of refried beans, 2 tablespoons of nacho cheese, ¼ cup of scrambled egg, and ½ cup of cooked ground beef.
8. Place a tostada over the fillings and add 2 tablespoons of sour cream, ½ cup of lettuce, ⅓ cup of cheese, 1 tablespoon of tomato, and 1 tablespoon of jalapeños.
9. Place a quartered tortilla on the fillings and then fold the bottom tortilla over the top with six or seven folds to seal the wrap.
10. Grill the wrap on the griddle, folded side down until browned, 2 to 3 minutes. Flip the wrap over and grill for an additional 2 to 3 minutes.
11. Remove and serve.

FINISH LINE PANCAKES

DIFFICULTY: Rookie | **PREP TIME:** 7 Minutes | **COOK TIME:** 5 Minutes | **SERVINGS:** 4

A DRIVER CROSSING THE finish line under the black-and-white checkered flag signifies the end of a NASCAR race. It's the view every team wants to see at the end of the day because the first driver there is the winner. With this classic breakfast dish of soft and fluffy pancakes topped with sweet black-and-white sprinkles, you'll be a winner, too! Drizzle with maple syrup—and enjoy!

8 ounces milk

2 large eggs

½ cup butter, melted, plus more for serving

2⅓ cups all-purpose flour

2 teaspoons baking powder

4 teaspoons white sprinkles, plus more for garnish

4 teaspoons black sprinkles, plus more for garnish

Maple syrup, for serving

1. In a medium bowl, combine the milk, eggs, and butter.
2. In a small bowl, combine the flour and baking powder.
3. Whisk in the dry ingredients to the wet ingredients. Once combined, stir in the sprinkles.
4. Prepare the griddle or cast-iron skillet on the grill for direct, medium heat cooking (350° to 400° F).
5. Apply a small amount of butter to the griddle. Once the butter melts, use a ⅓-cup measuring cup to add batter to the griddle. One batch will make eight or nine pancakes.
6. Grill the pancakes over medium heat until browned, flipping once, 3 to 4 minutes.
7. Serve with butter and syrup. Garnish with additional sprinkles.

VICTORY DONUTS

DIFFICULTY: Veteran | **PREP TIME:** 12 Minutes | **COOK TIME:** 12 Minutes | **SERVINGS:** 12

WHO DOESN'T LOVE A good donut? A NASCAR race isn't complete without "victory donuts," also known as when the winning driver spins their car around in circles to create a smoke show, often leaving behind circular, 8-shaped rubber marks on the track. Hendrick Motorsports teammates Chase Elliott in the No. 9 Chevrolet and Kyle Larson in the No. 5 Chevrolet are known to put on a good show for the fans while basking in the spoils of their successful day. These donuts are an irresistibly fluffy treat with their golden brown and slightly crisp exteriors.

2 cups flour

1 teaspoon baking soda

1 teaspoon cinnamon

¾ teaspoon baking powder

¼ teaspoon kosher salt

½ cup plus 2 tablespoons melted unsalted butter, divided

1 egg, beaten

½ cup light brown sugar

½ cup granulated sugar

½ cup whole milk

1 teaspoon vanilla extract

Nonstick spray

SUGAR MIXTURE

1 cup granulated sugar

¾ teaspoon cinnamon

EQUIPMENT

Gallon-size plastic bag

Mini donut pan

1. In a medium bowl, combine the flour, baking soda, cinnamon, baking powder, and salt.
2. In another medium bowl, combine 2 tablespoons of melted butter, the egg, brown sugar, granulated sugar, milk, and vanilla.
3. Add the dry ingredients to the wet ingredients and stir until combined.
4. To make the sugar mixture, in a small bowl, combine the granulated sugar and cinnamon. Set aside.
5. Spoon the batter in a gallon-size plastic bag. Using a pair of scissors, cut off a ½-inch corner. Doing so will allow you to pipe the batter into the donut molds.
6. Spray the donut pan molds with nonstick spray and then use the plastic bag with batter to fill each mold.
7. Prepare the grill for indirect, medium heat cooking (350° to 400° F).
8. Grill the donuts over indirect medium heat until the donuts are soft to the touch and cooked through, 10 to 12 minutes.
9. Remove from the grill. Remove the donuts from the mold. Dip the donuts in the remaining melted butter and toss in the sugar and cinnamon. Serve warm.

FUN FACT

Hendrick Motorsports has secured fourteen championships in the NASCAR Cup Series. Chase Elliott bolstered this total by claiming the championship in 2020. Kyle Larson further contributed by winning the championship in 2021.

MENARDS
HendrickCars.com
CAMARO
SportClips
TOYOTA
Kubota
CAMARO

SALADS

TRACKER
TOYOTA
CAMARO
TOYOTA
Mobil 1
Budweiser
TOYOTA
CAMARO
HOOTERS
CAMARO
RHEEM.COM
TOYOTA
20
16
4

GRILLED CAESAR SALAD

DIFFICULTY: Rookie | **PREP TIME:** 5 Minutes | **COOK TIME:** 3 Minutes | **SERVINGS:** 6 | **DIETARY:** GF

A PROPER MEAL ON race day is crucial for a driver before competing because they need to feel their best inside their race cars. That's why salads and chicken are popular choices in the garage area. Combine the two and you get this crunchy, creamy Grilled Caesar Salad. You and your favorite driver can't go wrong with this zesty dish that will keep you energized taking on the day ahead.

3 romaine hearts

Olive oil, for brushing

Kosher salt

Black pepper

Grated Parmesan cheese, for serving

Croutons, store-bought, for garnish

DRESSING

¾ cup mayonnaise

2 tablespoons freshly squeezed lemon juice

2 tablespoons Parmesan cheese

1 tablespoon olive oil

2 teaspoons Dijon mustard

2 teaspoons Worcestershire sauce

¼ teaspoon garlic powder

¼ teaspoon kosher salt

1. Cut the romaine hearts in half lengthwise through the root. Lightly brush with olive oil and season with salt and pepper.
2. In a small bowl, whisk together the dressing ingredients.
3. Prepare the grill for direct, medium heat cooking (350° to 400° F).
4. Grill the romaine, cut side down, over direct heat until the lettuce is marked, 1½ to 2 minutes. Flip and grill for 1 minute more.
5. Remove from the grill. Serve with the dressing and Parmesan cheese. Garnish with croutons.

SMOKED CHICKEN SALAD

DIFFICULTY: Veteran | **PREP TIME:** 15 Minutes | **COOK TIME:** 2 Hours | **SERVINGS:** 6 | **DIETARY:** GF

THIS SMOKED CHICKEN SALAD is a satisfying race day dish that has all the fun and flair of a tailgate party put into one showstopping dish. The smoky flavor will resonate in the protein-packed chicken while mixed with a tangy blend that only the flavor of a bold dressing of can bring.

1 whole chicken (4 to 5 pounds)

1 tablespoon olive oil

1 tablespoon BBQ rub (page 24)

RUB

1 cup mayonnaise

½ cup apple cider vinegar

2 celery stalks, chopped

½ Honeycrisp apple, cored and chopped

1 cup raisins

½ teaspoon kosher salt

¼ teaspoon black pepper

1. Prepare the grill for indirect, medium heat cooking, (350° to 400° F).
2. If using a charcoal grill, add three or four wood chunks directly to the lit coals once the coals have ashed over. If using a gas grill, add the wood chunks to a pouch made of aluminum foil with holes poked through the top. Put the pouch directly over a lit burner. Once the gas or charcoal grill begins to release white, wispy smoke, it's ready.
3. Coat the chicken with olive oil and season inside and out with the rub. Tuck the wings under the chicken.
4. Grill the chicken over indirect medium heat until the internal temperature of the breast reads 165° F with an instant-read thermometer, 1 hour 15 minutes to 1 hour 30 minutes.
5. Remove from the grill and allow to cool for 30 minutes.
6. Pull the meat from the chicken carcass, shred or cut into pieces, and place in a bowl. The chicken should yield 3 to 4 cups of meat. Either discard the skin and carcass or save for another use.
7. In a medium bowl, whisk the mayonnaise and apple cider vinegar, then stir in the remaining ingredients.
8. Toss the chicken with the salad dressing. For best results, cover and refrigerate for at least 2 hours before serving.

FUN FACT

Tony Stewart, a three-time NASCAR Cup Series Champion, also goes by his nickname, Smoke. The moniker came from early in Stewart's racing career when he admitted he didn't have good throttle control, which would cause smoke to come off his tires.

GRILLED SAUSAGE PASTA SALAD

DIFFICULTY: Veteran | **PREP TIME:** 12 Minutes | **COOK TIME:** 14 Minutes | **SERVINGS:** 8

THIS FRESH, LIGHT, AND perfectly Grilled Sausage Pasta Salad goes well with summertime NASCAR racing and tailgating. Fire up the grill to make your sausage, which will have the robust flavor bursting through its skin, right before it goes into the rest of the dish, which includes a rich cheesiness that makes every dish better and dressing flavors that makes everything pop.

3 Italian sausage links

½ pound penne pasta

½ red bell pepper, thinly sliced

½ green bell pepper, thinly sliced

2 tablespoons chopped fresh basil

Grated Parmesan cheese, for topping

DRESSING

1 tablespoon white wine vinegar

1½ teaspoons freshly squeezed lemon juice

1½ teaspoons grated Parmesan cheese

1 teaspoon dried Italian seasoning

½ teaspoon Dijon mustard

½ teaspoon honey

¼ cup extra-virgin olive oil

1. Prepare the grill for a two-zone fire with medium heat cooking (350° to 400° F).
2. Grill the sausage over direct medium heat for 4 minutes, flipping once. Move to indirect medium heat and continue to cook until the internal temperature of the sausage reads 155° F with an instant-read thermometer, 8 to 10 minutes more.
3. Remove the sausage from the grill, allow to cool slightly, cut in half lengthwise, then cut into ½-inch pieces. Set aside.
4. While the sausage is cooking, cook the pasta per the package instructions. When done, strain into a colander and run under cold water to stop cooking.
5. To make the dressing, in a small bowl, combine all the ingredients except the olive oil. Once combined, whisk and slowly drizzle in the olive oil until emulsified.
6. In a large bowl, toss the pasta, sausage, peppers, basil, and dressing. Cover and refrigerate for at least an hour.
7. Top with freshly grated Parmesan cheese prior to serving.

WATKINS GLEN GRILLED POTATO SALAD

DIFFICULTY: Veteran | **PREP TIME:** 10 Minutes | **COOK TIME:** 22 Minutes | **SERVINGS:** 8 | **DIETARY:** GF, V

A FAVORITE ON THE NASCAR schedule is the Watkins Glen Road course in the scenic Finger Lakes region of upstate New York. It's a high-speed course with elevation changes throughout and left and righthand corners that challenge drivers lap after lap. Unlike its namesake, this grilled potato salad is no challenge to make at your next NASCAR race day tailgate. In fact, it's so easy to prepare and eat that any racing driver would be asking for some in the victory lane!

2 pounds red potatoes, quartered

1 large sweet onion, quartered

1 teaspoon olive oil

1 teaspoon Italian seasoning

1 tablespoon chopped flat-leaf parsley

VINAIGRETTE

1 garlic clove, minced

2 teaspoons apple cider vinegar

1 teaspoon stone ground mustard

¼ teaspoon freshly squeezed lemon juice

¼ teaspoon kosher salt

2 tablespoons olive oil

1. Bring a large pot of water to a boil. Add the potatoes, return to a boil, and cook for 10 minutes. Strain the potatoes into a colander and rinse under cold water to stop them from cooking.
2. Prepare the grill for direct, medium heat cooking (350° to 400° F).
3. Pat dry the potatoes. Brush the potatoes and onion with the olive oil. Rub the potatoes with the Italian seasoning.
4. Grill the onions over direct medium heat for 12 to 14 minutes, turning several times. Remove from the grill.
5. Grill the potatoes over direct medium heat, cut side down, until marked, rotating once, 8 to 10 minutes. Remove from the grill.
6. To make the vinaigrette, in a small bowl, combine all the ingredients except the olive oil. Once combined, whisk and slowly drizzle in the olive oil until emulsified.
7. Chop the cooked onion and add to a medium bowl along with the potatoes. Toss with the vinaigrette and garnish with the parsley. Serve warm.

FUN FACT

Watkins Glen has been the site of a driver scoring their first career win in the NASCAR Cup Series four times. The most recent was Chase Elliott in 2018.

CORN, PINEAPPLE & BLACK BEAN SALAD

DIFFICULTY: Rookie | **PREP TIME:** 4 Minutes | **COOK TIME:** 5 Minutes | **SERVINGS:** 6 | **DIETARY:** GF, V

THIS VIBRANT SALAD STANDS on its own, either as a side dish or as the only thing you want to consume during your tailgate. In NASCAR, drivers often stand on their own when driving for a single car team, like Josh Berry at Wood Brothers Racing. Sometimes multiple drivers work together, like Todd Gilliland, Zane Smith, and Noah Gragson at Front Row Motorsports. The corn, pineapple, and black beans work together to make each bite like a refreshing pit stop.

- 3 canned pineapple rings
- One 15-ounce can whole corn kernels, drained
- One 15-ounce can black beans, drained and rinsed
- 1 tablespoon chopped fresh cilantro
- Juice of 1 lime
- 1 teaspoon dried cumin
- ¼ teaspoon kosher salt

1. Prepare the grill for direct, medium heat cooking (350° to 400° F).
2. Grill the pineapple rings over direct heat until marked, 4 to 5 minutes, flipping once.
3. Remove the pineapple from the grill and dice.
4. In a large bowl, combine the pineapple with the remaining ingredients.
5. For best results, cover and refrigerate for at least an hour prior to serving.

SIDES

SMOKED MAC & CHEESE

DIFFICULTY: Veteran | **PREP TIME:** 8 Minutes | **COOK TIME:** 50 Minutes | **SERVINGS:** 10

THERE ARE TIMES WHEN you might hear about how a driver smoked the competition. It's a compliment because it means they got the best of their rival, oftentimes leaving them in the dust on the track. This Smoked Mac & Cheese with not one but two great cheeses leaves all other dishes behind in the same exact manner. Charred, cheesy, and velvety smooth? Yes, please!

1 pound macaroni elbows

¼ cup butter, plus more for greasing

¼ cup flour

2½ cups whole milk

2 cups shredded cheddar cheese

2 cups shredded colby jack cheese

1 tablespoon ground mustard

1 teaspoon kosher salt

EQUIPMENT

Disposable foil pan or cast-iron skillet

Hickory smoking wood chunks or chips

1. Bring a large pot of water to a boil. Cook the macaroni according to the package instructions to al dente, about 6 minutes. Drain and set aside.
2. In a large skillet, melt the butter over medium heat. Whisk in the flour. Increase the heat to medium-high and whisk in the milk. Cook, stirring constantly, until the sauce thickens, 4 to 5 minutes.
3. Reduce the heat to medium-low and stir in the cheeses. Once the cheese has melted, stir in the mustard and salt.
4. In a large bowl, combine the cheese sauce and cooked macaroni.
5. Grease the bottom and sides of the foil pan.
6. Add the macaroni and cheese to the pan.
7. Prepare the grill for indirect, medium-high heat cooking (400° to 450° F).
8. If using a charcoal grill, add three or four wood chunks directly to the lit coals once the coals have ashed over. If using a gas grill, add the wood chunks to a pouch made of aluminum foil with holes poked through the top. Put the pouch directly over a lit burner. Once the gas or charcoal grill begins to release white, wispy smoke, it's ready.
9. Grill the macaroni and cheese over indirect medium-high heat until the cheese begins to brown, 35 to 40 minutes.
10. Remove and serve warm.

PIT CREW PIT BEANS

DIFFICULTY: Veteran | **PREP TIME:** 10 Minutes | **COOK TIME:** 1 Hour | **SERVINGS:** 8 | **DIETARY:** GF

NO RACE CAN BE run or won without a "pit crew," otherwise known as the people who service the car on pit road. They are among the most essential and valuable variables in racing. A good pit crew needs to be fast and efficient in changing tires, making adjustments, and adding fuel to race cars. These hearty beans are essential at any tailgate, making a quick, efficient side dish.

Two 28-ounce cans vegetarian baked beans

One 15-ounce can Great Northern beans, drained and rinsed

One 15-ounce can dark kidney beans, drained and rinsed

½ large sweet onion, diced

1 green bell pepper, diced

1 red bell pepper, diced

½ cup dark molasses

½ cup dark brown sugar

¼ cup yellow mustard

¼ cup honey

2 tablespoons BBQ rub (page 24)

1 tablespoon white vinegar

1 teaspoon ancho chili powder

EQUIPMENT

Large disposable foil pan

1. Combine the ingredients in the foil pan.
2. Prepare the grill for indirect, medium-low heat cooking (300° to 350° F).
3. Grill the beans over indirect heat for 1 hour, stirring occasionally.
4. Remove and serve warm.

FUN FACT

The art of a pit stop has evolved in so many ways over the seventy-five-year-plus history of NASCAR. But the most impressive is how fast the pit crew members can perform. Today, a winning pit stop of four tires and fuel can be performed in under 9 seconds!

BAKED POTATO BAR

DIFFICULTY: Rookie | **PREP TIME:** 5 Minutes | **COOK TIME:** 1 Hour | **SERVINGS:** 4

BE THE CREW CHIEF of your tailgate by choosing what goes on your baked potato with a fully loaded, flavor-packed Baked Potato Bar! Whether you're heaping on sour cream or cheddar cheese, the choices are endless, so enjoy crafting your potato just the way you want it, like customizing a race car. With so many winning toppings, this Baked Potato Bar is a champion!

Four 8 to 10-ounce russet potatoes

Olive oil, for coating

1 teaspoon kosher salt

½ teaspoon black pepper

TOPPINGS

Butter

Sour cream

Green onions or chives, chopped

Crumbled cooked bacon

Blue cheese crumbles

Shredded cheddar cheese

Shredded chicken

Pulled pork

Ranch dressing

BBQ sauce

Kosher salt

Black pepper

1. Place each potato in the middle of a piece of aluminum foil, roughly 10 by 12 inches in size.
2. Cover each potato with a thin coat of olive oil and season with salt and pepper.
3. Pierce each potato with a fork and then fold the foil sides up to wrap and seal the potato.
4. Prepare the grill for indirect, medium heat cooking (350° to 400° F).
5. Grill the potatoes over indirect medium heat for 45 minutes.
6. Remove the potatoes from the foil and place back on the grill.
7. Remove the potatoes from the grill once the skin begins to wrinkle and the potatoes are soft to the touch, 15 minutes more.
8. Using a knife, make a slit across the top of the potato. With your hands at both ends of the potato, push in slightly to expose the potato and make a pocket for fillings.

GRILLED CORN RIBS

DIFFICULTY: Veteran | **PREP TIME:** 15 Minutes | **COOK TIME:** 7 Minutes | **SERVINGS:** 6 | **DIETARY:** GF

NASCAR IS A SENSORY experience—nothing beats the smell of burnt rubber and gasoline! A tailgate is filled with smells, too, and one of the best comes from these Grilled Corn Ribs. By rubbing with a punch of chili and garlic powder and slathering with a kick of chipotle peppers, you'll have a delicious variation of corn on the cob. But the thing truly sets them apart is that they're bite-size and can be eaten with one hand. Now, toss 'em on the grill and get cooking!

4 ears corn

1 tablespoon olive oil

RUB

1 teaspoon ancho chili powder

1 teaspoon garlic powder

½ teaspoon cumin, ground

½ teaspoon dried orange peel, ground

½ teaspoon kosher salt

SAUCE

¼ cup mayonnaise

¼ cup sour cream

1 tablespoon chipotle peppers in adobo sauce, puréed

1 teaspoon freshly squeezed lime juice

Kosher salt

1. Prepare the grill with a two-zone fire for medium-high heat cooking (400° to 450° F).
2. Husk the corn and remove any silk.
3. Using a sharp knife, cut the ear of corn in half. Stand the cut pieces on their ends and cut in half again. Place the cut quarters on their cut side and cut in half. Each ear of corn yields eight "ribs."
4. In a small bowl, combine the rub ingredients. In a large bowl, toss the corn ribs with olive oil and cover evenly with rub.
5. In a small bowl, combine the sauce ingredients and set aside.
6. Grill the corn over direct, medium-high heat for 6 to 7 minutes, flipping once. The corn is done when the kernels are tender and charred. If the corn chars too fast, move to indirect heat to finish cooking.

GRILLED STEAKHOUSE FRIES

DIFFICULTY: Rookie | **PREP TIME:** 5 Minutes | **COOK TIME:** 15 Minutes | **SERVINGS:** 6 | **DIETARY:** GF

THESE FRIES ARE SO good that you'll want to eat them up quick—the same way Kyle Busch in his No. 8 Richard Childress Racing Chevrolet quickly eats up the competition on the racetrack! Busch has done so over 200 times in NASCAR, which makes him one of the sport's winningest drivers. These Grilled Steakhouse Fries are easy, fast to make, and go above and beyond what you might expect with some hotness from the garlic, onion, pepper, and chili sauce ingredients.

3 or 4 large russet potatoes (about 2½ to 3 pounds)

1 teaspoon olive oil

1 teaspoon kosher salt

1 teaspoon garlic powder

½ teaspoon onion powder

½ teaspoon black pepper

Grated Parmesan cheese, for topping

DIPPING SAUCE

¼ cup ketchup

¼ cup chili sauce

1. Bring a large pot of water to a boil.
2. Cut the potatoes into wedges by cutting the potato in half longways, then quarters, and then eighths. Each potato yields eight large fries.
3. Cook the fries in the boiling water for 5 minutes. Remove the fries and place in a large bowl of ice water to stop them from cooking.
4. Prepare the grill for direct, medium-high heat cooking (400° to 450° F).
5. Once the fries are cooled, transfer to a sheet pan and pat dry with paper towels.
6. Lightly brush the fries with olive oil and season all over with the salt, garlic, onion, and pepper.
7. In a small bowl, combine the dipping sauce ingredients.
8. Grill the fries over direct heat until browned, 8 to 10 minutes, flipping once.
9. Remove the fries from the grill, top with grated Parmesan, and serve with the dipping sauce.

FUN FACT

In 2010, Kyle Busch became the first driver to win all three NASCAR races in one weekend—Craftsman Truck, Xfinity, and Cup Series. Busch achieved this feat at Bristol Motor Speedway and then repeated it in 2017 at the same racetrack.

5550
EAGLE

MACARONI SALAD

DIFFICULTY: Rookie | **PREP TIME:** 15 Minutes | **SERVINGS:** 8 | **DIETARY:** GF

JUST LIKE HOW THE winning team performs the tradition of spraying champagne in the victory lane to make a race-winning day complete, this classic Macaroni Salad makes a tailgate complete. With this creamy, tangy, and satisfying Macaroni Salad, you'll get the classics, from celery and onion to the zesty taste of mustard and mayo. Friends will want extra helpings—guaranteed.

8 ounces elbow macaroni
1 cup mayonnaise
1 tablespoon pickle juice
1 tablespoon Dijon mustard
2 teaspoons white wine vinegar
¼ teaspoon red pepper flakes
⅛ teaspoon kosher salt
⅛ teaspoon black pepper
½ red bell pepper, diced
1 celery stock, diced
2 hard-boiled eggs, chopped
4 sweet gherkin pickles, diced

1. Cook the macaroni according to the package instructions. When done, strain into a colander and run under cold water to stop from cooking.
2. While the macaroni is cooking, in a large bowl, combine the mayonnaise, pickle juice, mustard, vinegar, red pepper flakes, salt, and black pepper.
3. Stir in the cooked macaroni and the remaining ingredients.
4. For best results, refrigerate for an hour before serving.

NEXT-GEN COWBOY CAVIAR

DIFFICULTY: Rookie | **PREP TIME:** 10 Minutes | **SERVINGS:** 8 | **DIETARY:** GF, V

STARTING WITH THE 2022 season, NASCAR introduced a brand-new race car, nicknamed "Next Gen," which stands for next generation of race cars. It looked different from what drivers had competed with in years past, and many parts and pieces were different, too. So, when you need something that just hits different, something to change up your get-together and the idea of a side dish, this cold bean salad is aptly named. It's a light, fresh, easy-to-make dish full of taste.

One 15-ounce can black beans, drained and rinsed

One 15-ounce can black-eyed peas, drained and rinsed

One 15-ounce can whole corn kernels, drained

1 red bell pepper, diced

1 large avocado, diced

½ cup chopped fresh cilantro

1 jalapeño, ribs and seeds removed, diced

¼ large red onion, diced

DRESSING

¼ cup extra-virgin olive oil

¼ cup red wine vinegar

Juice of 1 lime

1 garlic clove, minced

½ teaspoon kosher salt

¼ teaspoon dried cayenne pepper

¼ teaspoon black pepper

1. In a large bowl, combine the black beans, black-eyed peas, corn, pepper, avocado, cilantro, jalapeño, and onion.
2. In a small bowl, whisk together the dressing ingredients.
3. Toss the vegetables with the dressing and serve.

FUN FACT

Joey Logano won the NASCAR Cup Series Championship in the inaugural season of the Next-Gen race car. He went on to win the championship again two years later in 2024. With a total of three championships (2018, 2022, 2024), Logano has been the most successful driver in that category for Roger Penske.

GRILLED RANCH POTATOES

DIFFICULTY: Rookie | **PREP TIME:** 4 Minutes | **COOK TIME:** 20 Minutes | **SERVINGS:** 8 | **DIETARY:** GF, V

NASCAR RACE DAY REQUIRES some essentials such as tickets to the race, wearing your favorite driver's gear, hearing protection, and a scanner to listen to your favorite driver or the radio broadcast. Another essential, of course, is your race day meal. So, to be truly ready for race day, you need these Grilled Ranch Potatoes—a favorite for drivers filling up their lunch plates.

2 pound red potatoes, halved

2 tablespoons plus 1 teaspoon olive oil, divided

½ teaspoon kosher salt

¼ teaspoon black pepper

2 tablespoons Dijon mustard

1 garlic clove, minced

1. Bring a large pot of water to a boil. Add the potatoes, return to a boil, and cook for 10 minutes. Strain the potatoes into a colander and rinse under cold water to stop them from cooking.
2. Preheat the grill for direct, medium-high heat cooking (400° to 450° F).
3. Pat dry the potatoes with a paper towel, then lightly brush the potatoes with 1 teaspoon of olive oil and season with salt and pepper.
4. In a medium bowl, combine the remaining 2 tablespoons of olive oil, the mustard, and garlic.
5. Grill the potatoes over direct medium-high heat until browned and crispy, 10 to 12 minutes, flipping once.
6. Remove the potato from the grill and toss in the mustard mixture. Serve warm.

GRILLED SWEET POTATO WEDGES

DIFFICULTY: Rookie | **PREP TIME:** 4 Minutes | **COOK TIME:** 14 Minutes | **SERVINGS:** 4 | **DIETARY:** GF, V

GRILLING OF ANY KIND is a staple for a tailgate and NASCAR race day, whether you're at home or at the racetrack with your friends and family. Either way, it's worth taking time to enjoy the rich taste of these Grilled Sweet Potato Wedges before hearing the sweet sound of the announcer saying, "Drivers, start your engines!" These wedges are perfectly sweet, savory, and spiced.

2 large sweet potatoes

½ teaspoon kosher salt

½ teaspoon black pepper

½ teaspoon ground cinnamon

1 teaspoon olive oil

3 tablespoons unsalted butter, melted

2 teaspoons dark brown sugar

1. Cut each potato in half lengthwise, then cut each half again into quarters, and then the quarters into eight total wedges.
2. Bring a large pot of water to a boil. Add the potatoes, return to a boil, and cook for 4 minutes. Strain the potatoes into a colander and rinse under cold water to stop them from cooking.
3. Preheat the grill for direct, medium-high heat cooking (400° to 450° F).
4. Pat dry the potatoes with a paper towel.
5. In a small bowl, combine the salt, pepper, and cinnamon.
6. Lightly brush the potatoes with olive oil and season with the spice mixture.
7. Grill the potatoes over direct medium-high heat until browned and crispy, 8 to 10 minutes, flipping once.
8. In a small bowl, combine the melted butter and brown sugar. Brush the potatoes with the butter mixture several times during the last 2 minutes of cooking.
9. Remove from the grill and serve warm.

FUN FACT

The Pocono Raceway in Pocono, Pennsylvania, is the only track on the NASCAR schedule with three corners. That's because it's a triangle! Fittingly, the track's nickname is "The Tricky Triangle."

VICTORY VINEGAR SLAW

DIFFICULTY: Rookie | **PREP TIME:** 5 Minutes | **SERVINGS:** 8 | **DIETARY:** GF, V

NASCAR HOLDS RACES ON thirty-three racetracks across the United States and Mexico, which means there is a different type of race put on every weekend during the season. An intermediate racetrack is 1.5 miles in length or longer. A short track is 1 mile or shorter. A road course makes drivers go left and right. A superspeedway is usually over 2 miles and has the fastest speeds at close to 200 miles per hour. In that way, there are many ways to enjoy a nice Victory Vinegar Slaw on race day. Enjoy the sweetness of maple syrup mixed with the tangy, spicy strength of mustard and hot sauce.

¼ cup apple cider vinegar
2 teaspoons maple syrup
2 teaspoons Dijon mustard
1 garlic clove, minced
1 teaspoon celery seed
1 teaspoon vinegar hot sauce
¼ teaspoon kosher salt
½ cups extra-virgin olive oil
One 1-pound package coleslaw cabbage and carrot mix

1. In a small bowl, combine the apple cider vinegar, maple syrup, Dijon mustard, garlic, celery seed, hot sauce, and salt. Slowly whisk in the olive oil until the ingredients are emulsified.
2. Put the coleslaw mix in a large bowl and stir in the dressing.
3. For best results, cover and refrigerate for at least an hour.

MAINS

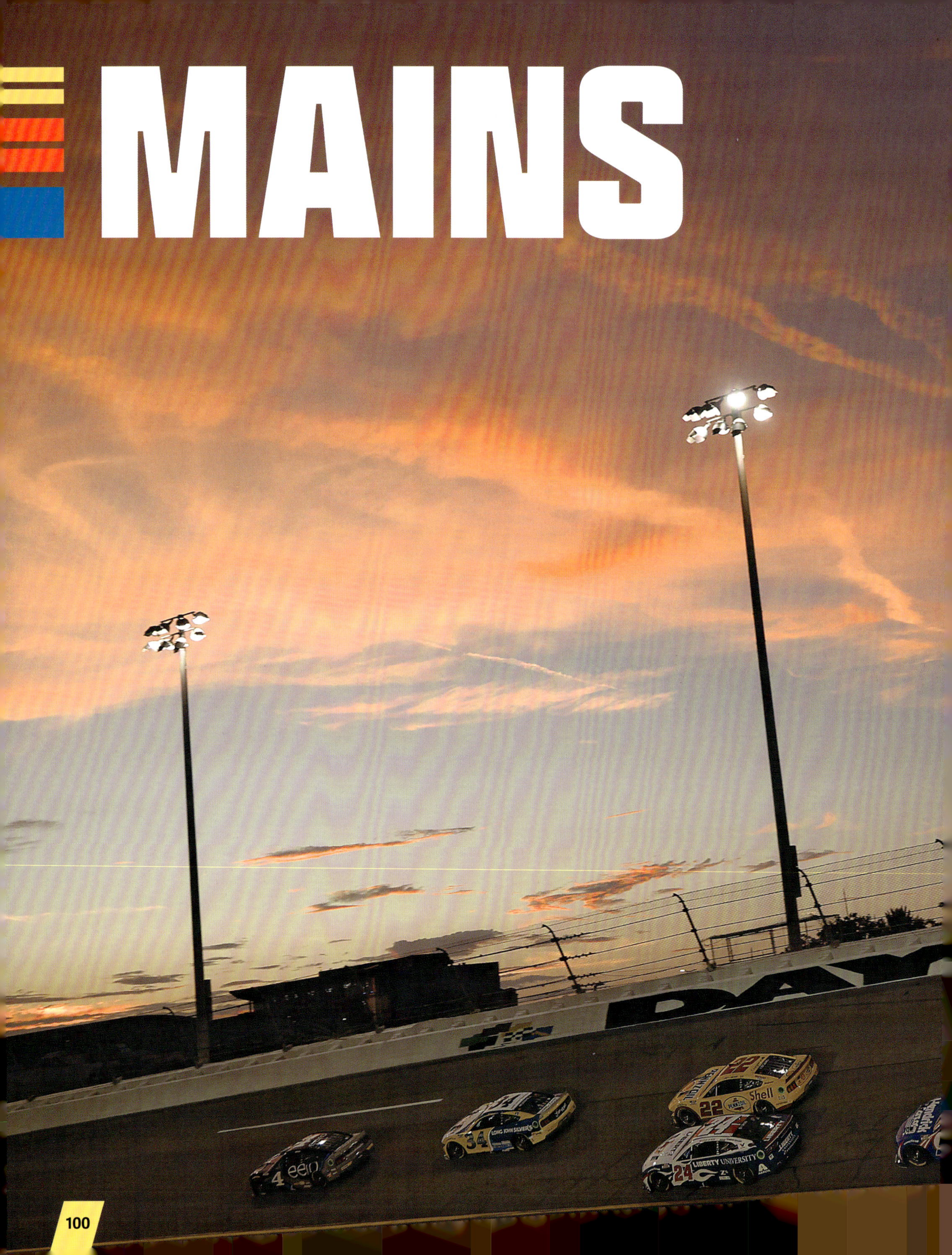

MENARDS
BREZTRI
PickleCAR
Cheddar's
FIFTH THIRD
INTERSTATE BATTERIES

KANSAS CITY BBQ CHICKEN LOLLIPOPS

DIFFICULTY: Champion | **PREP TIME:** 25 Minutes | **COOK TIME:** 1 Hour | **SERVINGS:** 4

NASCAR DRIVERS SOMETIMES HEAD to the Kansas Speedway, the 1.5-mile racetrack that opened in 2001 and had its first race won by Jeff Gordon in the No. 24 Hendrick Motorsports Chevrolet. Being in town means racers can enjoy good old Kansas City BBQ! If you want your race day tailgate to be the best, you must have a full-throttle BBQ dish like these juicy chicken lollipops. "Lollipop" refers to how the chicken legs look like the sweet treat with the meat pushed to one end—the easiest and most tender way to eat a chicken leg. These Kansas City BBQ Chicken Lollipops pack serious flavor and flair, with succulent chicken coated in a winning sweet and sticky glaze.

8 chicken legs

1 teaspoon olive oil

RUB

2 teaspoons kosher salt

1 teaspoon garlic powder

1 teaspoon paprika

1 teaspoon black pepper

GLAZE

1 cup store-bought BBQ sauce

½ cup butter, melted

1. Prepare the grill for indirect, low heat cooking (250° to 300° F).
2. With a sharp knife, cut around the bone and through the skin and tendons of a chicken leg just beneath the joint at the bone end.
3. Peel off the separated skin to expose the bone. With a paper towel for grip, remove any exposed tendons.
4. Slide the skin and meat toward the meaty side of the chicken leg so more bone is exposed and the chicken leg can stand vertical.
5. In a small bowl, combine the rub ingredients.
6. Lightly brush the chicken legs with olive oil and season with the rub.
7. In a heatproof container, combine the glaze ingredients and place on the grill over indirect heat to keep warm.
8. Grill the chicken over indirect low heat for 35 to 45 minutes.
9. Dip the chicken legs in the glaze and return to the grill.
10. Raise the grill temperature to medium heat cooking (350° to 400° F).
11. Continue to cook the chicken legs over indirect medium heat until the internal temperature reads 165° F with an instant-read thermometer, 10 to 15 minutes. Dip the legs in the glaze every 5 minutes until they finish cooking.
12. Remove from the grill and serve.

KANSAS SPEEDWAY

GRILLED PORK TENDERLOIN SLIDERS

DIFFICULTY: Veteran | **PREP TIME:** 10 Minutes | **COOK TIME:** 20 minutes | **SERVINGS:** 6

IT'S NOT A NASCAR race day tailgate until you fire up the grill! And there is no better reason to grill than with a nice pork tenderloin to feast on before settling in for some great racing action. Whether the juicy pork tenderloin is sliced thick or thin, these succulent Grilled Pork Tenderloin Sliders are great options that will have everyone reaching for seconds, thirds, and even fourths!

2 pork tenderloins (½ to 1 pound each)

1 teaspoon olive oil

RUB

2 teaspoons kosher salt

1 teaspoon onion powder

1 teaspoon garlic powder

1 teaspoon ground mustard

1 teaspoon ground black pepper

18 slider buns

9 slices cheddar cheese

1. Prepare the grill for a two-zone fire for medium heat cooking (350° to 400° F).
2. In a small bowl, combine the rub ingredients. Set aside.
3. Using a sharp knife, remove any excessive fat and silverskin from each tenderloin.
4. Lightly brush each tenderloin with olive oil and season with the rub.
5. Grill the tenderloins over direct medium heat for 2 minutes a side, 8 minutes total. Then move the tenderloins to indirect heat and continue to cook until the internal temperature reads 145° F with an instant-read thermometer, 10 to 12 minutes more.
6. Remove the tenderloins from the grill and allow to rest.
7. Grill the buns, cut side down, over direct heat until marked, about 1 minute.
8. Slice the tenderloins into 1-inch pieces. Top a bun with a slice of tenderloin, followed by a half slice of cheese.
9. Serve with your favorite condiments.

SUPERSPEEDWAY CHICKEN SANDWICHES

DIFFICULTY: Veteran | **PREP TIME:** 5 Minutes | **COOK TIME:** 8 minutes | **SERVINGS:** 8

RACES THAT TAKE PLACE on the Daytona International Speedway and the Talladega Superspeedway are classified as "superspeedway races" because of their high speeds and steep banking. There, you'll find fan favorites like Ricky Stenhouse Jr. in the No. 47 for Hyak Motorsports and William Byron in the No. 24 for Hendrick Motorsports battling wide-open and three-wide for victory. The winner will be looking for more than the trophy after hearing about these Superspeedway Chicken Sandwiches. As fast as the race cars go on the track, these sandos are just as quick to prepare and enjoy. And follow the step to grill those buns!

- 1½ pounds boneless, skinless chicken thighs
- ½ teaspoon olive oil
- 1 teaspoon ground cumin
- 1 teaspoon paprika
- ½ teaspoon kosher salt
- ¼ teaspoon black pepper
- 8 hamburger buns
- 1 jalapeño, diced, seeds and ribs removed
- ½ cup store-bought BBQ sauce
- Victory Vinegar Slaw, for topping (page 99)

1. Prepare the grill for direct, medium heat cooking (350° to 400° F).
2. Lightly brush the chicken with olive oil and season with cumin, paprika, salt, and pepper.
3. Grill the chicken over direct heat until the internal temperature of the chicken reads 165° F with an instant-read thermometer, 6 to 8 minutes, flipping once.
4. Grill the buns, cut side down, over direct medium heat until marked, about 1 minute. Remove from the grill and set aside.
5. Place the chicken in a medium bowl and, with two forks, shred into pieces. If available, the beater attachment on a stand mixer works best.
6. Stir in the jalapeño and BBQ sauce.
7. Top each bun with equal parts chicken and slaw.

FUN FACT

If you ever hear the phrase "free pass" during a NASCAR race, it means a driver has gotten one lap back. The free pass is awarded to the highest-running driver that is one or more laps down, and it helps keep them in the action!

ITALIAN-STYLE BEEF SANDWICHES

DIFFICULTY: Veteran | **PREP TIME:** 5 Minutes | **COOK TIME:** 2 Hours | **SERVINGS:** 8

THERE WILL BE JUMPING for joy when these sandwiches appear on the race day tailgate menu, because everyone will be making multiple pit stops to the picnic table for more of them. And that's what a good tailgate is all about: the anticipation of the race, friends, music, and dishes like this one. Race day fans can't get enough exploring all the food options and indulging in their favorites. These Italian-Style Beef Sandwiches are juicy, tender, and seasoned to perfection. And the winning part of this recipe? The smoked au jus.

3 to 4 pounds bottom round roast

RUB

1 teaspoon dried basil

2 teaspoons dried oregano

2 teaspoons garlic powder

1 teaspoon kosher salt

½ teaspoon black pepper

6 cups hot water

6 beef bouillon cubes

One 16-ounce jar giardiniera

8 Italian beef rolls

EQUIPMENT

9-by-13-inch disposable foil pan

Wire rack

Slow cooker

1. Prepare the grill for indirect, low heat cooking (250° to 300° F).
2. Remove any excessive fat from the surface of the roast.
3. In a small bowl, combine the rub ingredients, then season the roast all over with the rub.
4. Place the foil pan on the grill over indirect heat. Add the hot water and bouillon cubes to the foil pan. Put the wire rack over the pan and place the roast on the rack.
5. Grill the roast over indirect low heat until the internal temperature of the roast reads 125° F with an instant-read thermometer, 1 hour and 45 minutes to 2 hours.
6. Remove the roast from the grill, loosely cover with foil, and allow to rest for 30 to 45 minutes.
7. Place the juice from the foil pan in the slow cooker and set to warm.
8. Using a sharp knife, or a meat slicer, if available, thinly slice the meat.
9. Top the rolls with sliced meat and giardiniera. Serve with the warm juice for dipping.

FUN FACT

NASCAR introduced a playoff format to the sport for the first time in 2004, aligning it with other major sporting leagues that similarly crown their champions. The playoff format has evolved over the years, but the system has consistently produced many memorable moments.

BIG BILL'S GRIDDLED CATFISH NUGGETS

DIFFICULTY: Veteran | **PREP TIME:** 8 Minutes | **COOK TIME:** 6 Minutes | **SERVINGS:** 4

THE FOUNDER OF NASCAR was famously known as "Big" Bill France—a one-of-a-kind man who also founded a one-of-a-kind racetrack in Talladega Superspeedway. Race weekend at Talladega is never complete without its traditional catfish fry. But take it a step further by including the zing from lemons, ones that need some time on the grill, as a zesty condiment.

1 cup flour, divided

1 teaspoon kosher salt

1 teaspoon black pepper

2 large eggs, beaten

½ cup cornmeal

2 teaspoon paprika

2 teaspoon garlic

1 pound fresh catfish nuggets

Vegetable oil, for frying

2 lemons, quartered

Fresh Italian parsley, chopped, for serving

1. Prepare a breading station with three medium shallow bowls. In the first bowl, combine ½ cup of flour, the salt, and pepper. In the second bowl, put the beaten eggs. In the third bowl, combine the remaining ½ cup of flour, the cornmeal, paprika, and garlic.
2. Prepare the griddle, or a cast-iron skillet on the grill, for medium heat cooking (350° to 400° F).
3. Pat dry the catfish with a paper towel. Dredge the catfish in the flour, shaking off any excess. Then dredge the catfish in the egg wash. Allow any excess egg to drip off the catfish, and then dredge in the cornmeal mixture.
4. Apply a thin layer of oil to the griddle.
5. Grill the catfish over direct medium heat until golden brown and the internal temperature of the catfish reads 145° F with an instant-read thermometer, 5 to 6 minutes, flipping once.
6. During the last 2 minutes of cooking, grill the lemons over direct heat, flesh side down, until marked.
7. Remove the catfish and lemon from the grill. Squeeze the grilled lemons over the catfish. Garnish with parsley and serve.

FUN FACT

The best place to enjoy these crispy nuggets is in the open-air hospitality area in the infield, fittingly known as "Big Bill's."

DARLINGTON PULLED PORK

DIFFICULTY: Champion | **PREP TIME:** 12 Minutes | **COOK TIME:** 9 Hours | **SERVINGS:** 12 | **DIETARY:** GF

ANY RACE FAN KNOWS that pulled pork is a must-have at a tailgate. The southeast, particularly in the Carolinas, has made pulled pork a staple, using vinegar sauce as a popular ingredient. Darlington Raceway, set in South Carolina, is a fan-favorite racetrack where visitors are no strangers to pulled pork—because pulled pork sandwiches are sold at this racetrack! If you want to feel like a champ, this savory, sweet, and bold recipe for pulled pork is a real crowd-pleaser!

One 6- to 8-pound bone-in pork butt

RUB

2 tablespoons dark brown sugar

2 tablespoons paprika

2 tablespoons cumin

1 teaspoon garlic

1 teaspoon kosher salt

1 teaspoon black pepper

1 teaspoon ground mustard

½ teaspoon celery seed

½ teaspoon ancho chili powder

VINEGAR SAUCE

2 cups apple cider vinegar

2 tablespoons dark brown sugar

1 tablespoon vinegar hot sauce

1 teaspoon red pepper flakes

½ teaspoon kosher salt

½ teaspoon black pepper

EQUIPMENT

Applewood chunks or chips

1. In a small bowl, combine the rub ingredients.
2. Prepare the grill for indirect, low heat cooking (250° to 300° F).
3. If using a charcoal grill, add three or four wood chunks directly to the lit coals once the coals have ashed over. If using a gas grill, add the wood chunks to a pouch made of aluminum foil with holes poked through the top. Put the pouch directly over a lit burner. Once the gas or charcoal grill begins to release white, wispy smoke, it's ready.
4. Generously cover the pork shoulder with rub.
5. Grill the pork shoulder, fat cap down, over indirect heat until the internal temperature reads 165° F with an instant-read thermometer, 5 to 6 hours.
6. Remove the pork shoulder from the grill and wrap tightly in two layers of aluminum foil.
7. Return the pork to the grill and continue to cook until the internal temperature reads 203° F with an instant-read thermometer, 2 to 3 hours more.
8. Remove the pork from the grill and place in an insulated cooler to rest for at least 2 hours (up to 4).
9. In a small saucepan, combine the sauce ingredients and bring to a boil. Reduce the heat to low and simmer until the sugar is dissolved, about 4 minutes.
10. When ready to serve, remove the pork shoulder from the foil. Remove the bone. Then, using either two forks or your hands wearing insulated gloves, gently pull the pork into pieces.
11. Serve with the sauce.

PLAYOFF PARTY PORK RIBS

DIFFICULTY: Champion | **PREP TIME:** 10 Minutes | **COOK TIME:** 3 Hours | **SERVINGS:** 8

IT'S TIME FOR A celebration when a team makes the playoffs to compete for the NASCAR Cup Series championship. A season's worth of work pays off to get to the final stretch, where the biggest prize is on the line—the "Bill France Cup." When you're able to make these flavor-packed, super-sticky, and crispy BBQ pork ribs in a faster-than-normal cook, it'll feel like your tailgate has turned into a celebratory party—and a flavor party in your mouth, too! Party on!

2 racks baby back ribs

RUB

4 teaspoons dark brown sugar

4 teaspoons paprika

1 teaspoon kosher salt

1 teaspoon chili powder

1 teaspoon ground mustard

½ teaspoon cayenne pepper

½ teaspoon black pepper

SAUCE

1 cup store-bought BBQ sauce

¼ cup unsalted butter

2 tablespoons vinegar-based hot sauce

1 tablespoon dark brown sugar

1 tablespoon maple syrup

EQUIPMENT

Cherry wood chunks or chips

Foil pan

1. Prepare the grill for indirect, low heat cooking (250° to 300° F).
2. If using a charcoal grill, add three or four wood chunks directly to the lit coals once the coals have ashed over. If using a gas grill, add the wood chips to a pouch made of aluminum foil with holes poked through the top. Put the pouch directly over a lit burner. Once the gas or charcoal grill begins to release white, wispy smoke, it's ready.
3. Remove the membrane from the back of both racks of ribs, then cut the racks through the meaty sections into individual ribs.
4. In a small bowl, combine the rub ingredients, then coat the ribs with the rub.
5. Smoke the ribs over indirect low heat for 90 minutes, flipping once.
6. In a small pan, warm the sauce ingredients.
7. Place the ribs in the foil pan. Coat with the sauce and cover tightly with aluminum foil.
8. Return the foil pan to the grill and continue to cook over indirect low heat for an hour flipping the ribs halfway through.
9. Remove the foil cover from the pan and continue to cook until the internal temperature of the pork meat reads 203° F with an instant-read thermometer, about 30 minutes more.
10. Remove from the grill and serve.

CHICAGO-STYLE HOT DOGS

DIFFICULTY: Rookie | **PREP TIME:** 5 Minutes | **COOK TIME:** 5 Minutes | **SERVINGS:** 8

THERE IS NO BETTER dish than a Chicago-Style Hot Dog to go with the Chicago street course race. NASCAR races around the streets of downtown Chicago, turning left and right and past some of the city's most recognizable landscapes in a 2.2-mile circuit. This hot dog, inspired by those found in the Windy City, delivers as many twists and turns of flavor that make it a classic—and 23XI Racing driver Bubba Wallace–approved. The best part is dragging it through the garden with so many bold, flavorful condiments and finally chowing down!

8 all-beef hot dogs

8 poppy seed hot dog buns

TOPPINGS

8 pickle spears

2 tomatoes, cut into 8 wedges

Sports peppers

Yellow mustard

1 medium yellow onion, chopped

Pickle relish

Celery salt

1. Prepare the griddle or cast-iron skillet on a grill for direct, medium heat cooking (350° to 400° F).
2. Grill the hot dogs over direct medium heat until warmed through, 4 to 5 minutes.
3. Add the buns to the grill, cut side down, during the last minute of cooking.
4. Remove the buns and hot dogs from the grill and place a hot dog in each bun.
5. Top each hot dog with a pickle spear, two tomato wedges, sport peppers, mustard, onion, relish, and celery salt.

NOTE: For authentic Chicago relish, add a few drops of blue food coloring to the relish to turn it neon green. Also, if you can't find sports peppers at your local grocery, substitute chopped pepperoncini.

ALL-STAR SKIRT STEAK TACO BAR

DIFFICULTY: Veteran | **PREP TIME:** 15 Minutes | **COOK TIME:** 6 Minutes | **SERVINGS:** 8

THE NASCAR ALL-STAR RACE is one of the most exciting events of the season. It's invitation-only for drivers who have earned eligibility based on the rules of the season, and though it doesn't award points since it's a specialty event, it does pay $1 million! When a taco bar features the mouthwatering flavors of skirt steak, it makes for an all-star eating event. Your taco will be upgraded when pairing this tender, thin, rich meat with so many other delicious ingredients.

RUB

2 teaspoons chili powder

1 teaspoon ground cumin

½ teaspoon kosher salt

¼ teaspoon black pepper

1½ pounds skirt steak

1 teaspoon olive oil

Twelve 8-inch flour tortillas

TOPPINGS

Grilled salsa (page 14)

1 can black beans, drained

Fresh store-bought guacamole

Shredded romaine lettuce head

Grape tomatoes, chopped

Green onions, green part only, chopped

Pickled jalapeños, sliced

3 limes, quartered

1 bunch fresh cilantro, chopped

Cotija cheese, crumbled

1. In a small bowl, combine the rub ingredients.
2. Remove any excessive fat and silverskin from the skirt steak. Lightly brush the skirt steak with oil and season all over with the rub.
3. Prepare the grill for direct, high heat cooking (500° to 550° F).
4. Grill the steak over direct high heat until the internal temperature reads 125° F with an instant-read thermometer, 4 to 5 minutes, flipping once.
5. Remove the steak from the grill and allow to rest a few minutes.
6. While the steak rests, grill the tortillas over direct heat for 30 seconds, flipping once. Remove and keep warm in aluminum foil.
7. Cut the steak into bite-size pieces and set up a serving bar with the remaining ingredients.

FUN FACT

Joey Logano was the 2016 and 2024 NASCAR All-Star Race winner.

SHORT TRACK SMASHBURGERS

DIFFICULTY: Veteran | **PREP TIME:** 5 Minutes | **COOK TIME:** 4 Minutes | **SERVINGS:** 4

A "SHORT TRACK" IN NASCAR is any track that is less than 1 mile in length. And when you put forty drivers in a small space, it sometimes takes hitting a driver's bumper to move them out of the way for a position. It's called the bump-and-run. A tasty smashburger gets the job done when it comes to satisfying appetite, and these Short Track Smashburgers are crispy, juicy, and perfect.

1½ pounds 80/20 ground chuck
Canola oil, for frying
2 teaspoons kosher salt
1 teaspoon black pepper
8 slices cheddar cheese
8 slices pepper jack cheese
8 hamburger buns

EQUIPMENT

Burger press

1. Form the ground chuck into eight equal balls, each about 3 ounces.
2. Prepare the griddle or a cast-iron skillet on the grill for direct, medium-high heat cooking (400° to 450° F).
3. Apply a thin coating of oil to the griddle. Place the ground chuck balls on the griddle and smash each flat with the burger press. When pressing down, hold the press for a few seconds before sliding it off the patty. Season the patties with the salt and pepper.
4. Grill the patties over direct medium-high heat until cooked through, 3 to 4 minutes, flipping once.
5. Once flipped, top each burger with a slice of cheddar and pepper jack cheese, place the top of each bun, cut side down, on the cheese, and then the bottom bun, cut side up, on the top bun. This allows the buns to steam while the burger finishes cooking.
6. Once done, remove the bottom bun from each stack and top with the cooked smashburger. Serve with your favorite condiments.

CHECKERED FLAG CHEESY GRILLED TACOS

DIFFICULTY: Champion | **PREP TIME:** 25 Minutes | **COOK TIME:** 9 Minutes | **SERVINGS:** 4

THE CHECKERED FLAG FLIES to mark the end of a race, and every driver wants to be the first one to drive underneath it to claim the victory. It also marks the end of a driver's qualifying lap. These Checkered Flag Cheesy Grilled Tacos are in the fast lane to a flavor finish. They're a unique twist on an easy, handheld favorite and bring together classic tastes with cheese and a smoky crunch.

CHIPOTLE SAUCE

2 tablespoons chipotles in adobo sauce, puréed

2 tablespoons olive oil

4 teaspoons beef broth

4 teaspoons lime juice

2 teaspoons brown sugar

2 teaspoons ancho chili powder

1 teaspoon cumin

1 teaspoon garlic

¼ teaspoon salt

2 pounds English-cut beef short ribs, butterflied*

1 teaspoon vegetable oil, for brushing

2 teaspoons kosher salt

1 teaspoon freshly ground black pepper

1 red onion, thinly sliced

6 cups shredded Mexican-style cheese

16 street taco–style flour tortillas

1. In a small bowl, combine the chipotle sauce ingredients. Transfer to a squeeze bottle and set aside.
2. Prepare the griddle for direct, medium-high heat cooking (450° to 500° F).
3. Lightly brush the ribs with oil and season with salt and pepper.
4. Grill the ribs over direct medium-high heat until the internal temperature reads 125° F with an instant-read thermometer, flipping once, about 4 minutes total. Remove and cut the meat into ½-inch pieces.
5. Lightly coat the griddle with oil. Cook the red onions until softened and marked, 2 to 3 minutes. Remove and set aside.
6. Cook the tortillas on the griddle for 30 seconds, flipping once.
7. Place four ¼ cups of shredded cheese on the flat top, leaving plenty of space in between.
8. Place a tortilla on each mound of cheese. Top each tortilla with the meat, onions, sauce, and cheese. With a spatula, fold the cheese and tortilla over on itself. Cook for 15 seconds, then flip the tortilla over. Grill for an additional 15 seconds, then remove.
9. Repeat with the remaining tortillas. Serve with any remaining sauce.

*Place the short rib on a cutting board with the bone down, and, using a sharp knife, make a horizontal cut just over the bone from the left to the meaty right, stopping just short of the end. Open the short rib to lie flat, like a book. Make a second horizontal cut through the middle of the remaining meat section, stopping just before the end. Spread flat. When done, the entire piece of short rib, including the bone, should be of roughly the same thickness.

PIZZA GRILLED CHEESE

DIFFICULTY: Rookie | **PREP TIME:** 5 Minutes | **COOK TIME:** 5 Minutes | **SERVINGS:** 6

WHEN ONE FAVORITE DISH isn't enough, simply combine them! It's like taking NASCAR racing back to the historic North Wilkesboro Speedway—a cornerstone of the sport since its early days, sitting in the heart of the mountains of North Carolina where racing was born. The area produced many of the sport's legends, such as Junior Johnson and Benny Parsons. When you take a bite of this melty, crispy Pizza Grilled Cheese, you'll find it just as legendary in its taste.

12 slices white bread

2 tablespoons mayonnaise

½ cup store-bought pizza sauce

One 6-ounce package sliced pepperoni

3 cups shredded mozzarella cheese

2 teaspoons dried oregano

1. Prepare the griddle or a cast-iron skillet on the grill for direct, medium heat cooking (350° to 400° F).
2. Spread a thin layer of mayonnaise on one side of each slice of bread. Stack two slices of bread together, mayonnaise side to mayonnaise side.
3. On the top slice of each bread, equally add the pizza sauce, half of the pepperoni slices, the cheese, remaining pepperoni slices, and the oregano.
4. Place the pizza-loaded bread slice on the griddle, with the mayonnaise side down, and then top it with the remaining slice of bread, with the mayonnaise side up to form the sandwich.
5. Griddle over medium until the bread turns golden brown and the cheese has melted, 4 to 5 minutes.

FUN FACT

While Joe Gibbs is a winner and champion owner in NASCAR, he is also a winner and Super Bowl champion coach in the NFL with the Washington Commanders.

VALLEY OF THE SUN SOUTHWEST WRAP

DIFFICULTY: Veteran | **PREP TIME:** 10 Minutes | **COOK TIME:** 10 Minutes | **SERVINGS:** 8

NOT EVERY RACETRACK HAS a nickname. But Phoenix Raceway is worthy of one after becoming one of the most state-of-the-art facilities on the NASCAR circuit after a multimillion-dollar modernization project of the facility to upgrade the experience for competitors and race fans. Make sure you treat yourself to this upgrade of a wrap, with its tender chicken, melted cheese, and fresh veggies, wrapped in a tortilla. It's stuffed with flavor and easy to enjoy on the go!

RUB

½ teaspoon chili powder

½ teaspoon brown sugar

¼ teaspoon kosher salt

¼ teaspoon dried paprika

¼ teaspoon dried oregano

¼ teaspoon garlic powder

¼ teaspoon black pepper

¼ teaspoon cayenne pepper

SAUCE

½ cup ranch dressing

1 teaspoon dried chipotle pepper powder

¼ teaspoon hot sauce

1½ pounds boneless, skinless chicken breasts

½ teaspoon olive oil

8 extra-large flour tortillas

4 cups shredded cheddar cheese

1 cup whole corn kernels

One 15-ounce can black beans, drained and rinsed

Shredded romaine lettuce, for topping

Grape tomatoes, quartered, for topping

1. In a small bowl, combine the rub ingredients. In another small bowl, combine the sauce ingredients. Set aside.
2. Prepare the grill for direct, medium heat cooking (350° to 400° F).
3. Lightly brush the chicken breasts with olive oil and season all over with the rub.
4. Grill the chicken breasts over direct medium heat until the internal temperature of the breast reads 165° F with an instant-read thermometer, depending on size, 8 to 10 minutes. Flip once.
5. Remove the chicken breasts from the grill and, on a cutting board, cut into bite-size pieces.
6. Place a tortilla on a clean work surface and fill the middle with chicken, cheese, corn, black beans, lettuce, tomatoes, and sauce.
7. Fold the tortilla sides in first, then roll the tortilla forward to make the wrap, tucking the sides in as you go. Repeat for the remaining tortillas.
8. Slice in half and serve.

FUN FACT

"The Valley of the Sun" refers to the Phoenix metropolitan area, where the Phoenix Raceway is located.

GREEN-WHITE-CHECKERED QUESADILLAS

DIFFICULTY: Veteran | **PREP TIME:** 5 Minutes | **COOK TIME:** 12 Minutes | **SERVINGS:** 8

NASCAR SOMETIMES NEEDS MORE laps than what is in the advertised race distance to finish a race. When that happens, it's called overtime, or a green-white-checkered finish. In that event, the first lap is the green flag lap, the next lap is the white flag lap, and then the checkered flag flies. When your tailgate needs more pizzazz because your appetite hasn't been satisfied, look no further: A crispy, Green-White-Checkered Quesadilla is a top contender. It's warm, filling, and packed with protein from its juicy, seasoned chicken. Add zesty toppings for even more flavor!

1½ pounds boneless, skinless chicken thighs

1 teaspoon olive oil, divided

1½ teaspoons paprika

1 teaspoon kosher salt

½ teaspoon black pepper

Eight 8-inch flour tortillas

4 green onions, thinly sliced

½ cup white onion, minced

4 cups Mexican-style shredded cheese

Fresh salsa, for serving

Sour cream, for serving

1. Prepare the grill for direct, medium heat cooking (350° to 400° F).
2. Lightly brush the chicken with ½ teaspoon of olive oil and season with the paprika, salt, and pepper.
3. Grill the chicken over direct heat until the internal temperature of the chicken reads 165° F with an instant-read thermometer, 6 to 8 minutes, flipping once.
4. Remove, allow to cool slightly, then chop into pieces.
5. Lightly brush one side of the tortillas with the remaining ½ teaspoon of olive oil and place oil side down on a cutting board.
6. Evenly divide the chicken, green onions, white onion, and cheese on one half of each tortilla. Fold the other half over the toppings.
7. Grill the quesadillas over direct medium until the tortilla is marked and the cheese has melted, 3 to 4 minutes, flipping once.
8. Remove the quesadilla from the grill, cut into pieces, and serve with salsa and sour cream.

MARTINSVILLE HOT DOGS

DIFFICULTY: Rookie | **PREP TIME:** 5 Minutes | **COOK TIME:** 13 Minutes | **SERVINGS:** 8

MARTINSVILLE SPEEDWAY IS A half-mile paperclip-shaped racetrack set in Virginia, and it's the oldest track on the schedule as the only venue to have hosted a race every year since NASCAR's inception in 1947. Over the years, it has become a driver and fan favorite for its action-packed races. Another reason it's a fan favorite is the track's very own hot dog—famous within the sport! Known for its bright pink color, the Martinsville Hot Dog can be consumed in a variety of ways with its many ingredients, but a full flavor burst means it contains the works!

RED SLAW

¼ cup apple cider vinegar

¼ cup ketchup

1 teaspoon sugar

¼ teaspoon hot sauce

Kosher salt

2 cups cabbage and carrot coleslaw mix

One 15-ounce can beanless chili

Vegetable oil, for greasing

1 large yellow onion, sliced

8 Southern-style red hot dogs

8 hot dog buns

Yellow mustard

1 medium white onion, chopped

EQUIPMENT

Basting dome or lid

1. In a small bowl, whisk together the apple cider vinegar, ketchup, sugar, and hot sauce. Add salt to taste. Put the coleslaw mix in a medium bowl and stir in the dressing. Set aside.
2. In a small pot, warm the chili over medium-low heat.
3. Prepare the griddle or cast-iron skillet on a grill for direct, medium heat cooking (350° to 400° F).
4. Spread a thin layer of oil on the griddle and cook the onions over direct heat until soft and translucent, 7 to 8 minutes.
5. While the onions are cooking, cook the hot dogs over direct heat until cooked through, 4 to 5 minutes.
6. During the last few minutes of the hot dogs cooking and working in batches, add four buns to the top of the onions. Squirt a small amount of water on the griddle next to the buns and cover with the basting dome to steam the buns for no more than a minute.
7. Remove the buns and hot dogs from the grill. Place a hot dog in each bun, then top with mustard, chili, slaw, and onions.

FUN FACT

Martinsville Hot Dogs are sold at the infield hot dog stand. It is common to see drivers and team members in line, keeping a tally of how many hot dogs they've eaten during race weekend!

DESSERTS

OVERTIME DESSERT TACOS

DIFFICULTY: Rookie | **PREP TIME:** 2 Minutes | **COOK TIME:** 1 Minute | **SERVINGS:** 6 | **DIETARY:** V

THE CHANCE TO HAVE dessert means getting more of your meal to enjoy. The same applies in NASCAR when a race goes into overtime to determine the finish, which means there are more laps of racing to enjoy. These Overtime Dessert Tacos are super easy to make and are brimming with a tantalizing mix of crunchiness from the tortilla and a sweetness from the sugar and strawberries. Finish it all off with a generous drizzle of chocolate syrup. Every tailgate needs this sweet treat!

Six 8-inch flour tortillas

One 3.75-ounce jar sugar and cinnamon

Canola oil, for frying

TOPPINGS

Vanilla ice cream

Quart fresh strawberries, chopped

Chocolate syrup

EQUIPMENT

Taco rack

1. Prepare the griddle, or a cast-iron skillet on the grill, for direct, medium heat cooking (350° to 400° F).
2. Spread a thin layer of sugar and cinnamon on a large plate.
3. Apply a generous amount of oil to the griddle and then cook the tortilla on the oil for 10 to 15 seconds a side. Remove the tortilla from the griddle and dredge in the sugar and cinnamon. Shake off any excessive sugar and then place the tortilla in the taco rack. Repeat with the remaining tortillas.
4. Fill each tortilla with ice cream and strawberries. Top with chocolate syrup.

SPICY CANDIED BACON

DIFFICULTY: Rookie | **PREP TIME:** 4 Minutes | **COOK TIME:** 30 Minutes | **SERVINGS:** 6 | **DIETARY:** GF

NO TAILGATE IS COMPLETE without bacon, one of the most popular treats in NASCAR for fans and drivers alike! Smithfield Foods once had a bacon-fueled slogan on driver Aric Almirola's race car. Noah Gragson once drove a bacon-themed race car for his sponsor. You can't go wrong with bacon, and turning it into this sweet, spicy treat will make you a victorious race day host.

8 slices bacon

¼ cup dark brown sugar

1 tsp dried chipotle peppers

EQUIPMENT

Large grill pan

1. Line the grill pan with aluminum foil. Place the bacon strips on the foil side by side.
2. In a small bowl, combine the brown sugar and the chipotle pepper.
3. Prepare the grill for indirect medium heat cooking (350°–400° F).
4. Grill the bacon over indirect medium heat for 15 minutes.
5. Remove the pan from the grill, flip the bacon, and sprinkle with the sugar mixture.
6. Continue to cook the bacon over indirect heat for another 15 to 20 minutes, or until your desired level of doneness. Remove and allow to cool before serving.

FUN FACT

The Coca-Cola 600 at Charlotte Motor Speedway is the longest race on the NASCAR schedule, consisting of 400 laps and spanning 600 miles. A long day prompts many drivers and teams to stock up on food and snacks to enjoy during the event.

PHOENIX CHAMPIONSHIP CHOCOLATE GRILLED BANANAS

DIFFICULTY: Rookie | **PREP TIME:** 10 Minutes | **COOK TIME:** 15 Minutes | **SERVINGS:** 4 | **DIETARY:** V

THE NASCAR CUP SERIES championship trophy is typically hosted at the Phoenix Raceway, which moved into the rotation of venues that host NASCAR Championship Weekend in 2020. Although it is only 1 mile in length and labeled as a short track, Phoenix is a fast track with multiple lanes that allow drivers to fan out and run three- and four-wide on the frontstretch. This colorful dessert is a fast track for a successful tailgating event, known for its spoonfuls of warmly grilled bananas, creamy peanut butter, and crunchy chocolate bar, nuts, and rainbow sprinkles.

4 bananas

½ cup creamy peanut butter

1 chocolate bar, chopped

¼ cup chopped nuts

Rainbow sprinkles, for topping

1. Using a knife, cut a slit down the center of each banana without cutting all the way through the bottom. Grasp both ends of the banana and push inward to create a pocket in the flesh.
2. Fill the pocket of each banana with equal parts peanut butter and chocolate. Top with the nuts.
3. Prepare the grill for indirect, medium heat cooking (350° to 400° F).
4. Grill the bananas over indirect medium heat until the peel has darkened and the banana softened, 12 to 15 minutes.
5. Remove, top with sprinkles, and serve.

BROWN SUGAR BLUEBERRY COBBLER

DIFFICULTY: Veteran | **PREP TIME:** 10 Minutes | **COOK TIME:** 1 Hour | **SERVINGS:** 6 | **DIETARY:** V

IT DOESN'T GET ANY better than NASCAR racing and cobbler! The two go splendidly together—a great American sport with a great American dessert. Enjoy NASCAR race day with this warm, Brown Sugar Blueberry Cobbler. Its juicy blueberries and crunchy pecans are one sweet combo!

1¼ cups granulated sugar

1 cup self-rising flour

1 cup whole milk

¾ cup unsalted butter, divided and melted

3 cups frozen blueberries, thawed

1 teaspoon vanilla extract

2 teaspoons cornstarch

2 tablespoons granulated sugar

¾ cup brown sugar

¾ cup chopped pecans

EQUIPMENT

9-by-13-inch disposable foil pan

1. In a medium bowl, whisk together the sugar, flour, milk and ½ cup of melted butter.
2. In another medium bowl, gently combine the blueberries, vanilla, cornstarch, and granulated sugar.
3. Grease the foil pan, then add three-fourths of the blueberry mixture. Top with the batter followed by the remaining blueberries.
4. Prepare the grill for indirect, medium heat cooking (350° to 400° F).
5. Cook the cobbler over indirect medium heat for 45 minutes.
6. While the cobbler is cooking, in a small bowl, combine the remaining ¼ cup of butter, the brown sugar, and pecans.
7. Top the cobbler with the pecan mixture. Cook until the top is golden brown, about another 15 minutes.
8. Remove from the grill and serve.

FUN FACT

Joey Logano still enjoys how sweet it is to hold the record as the youngest winner ever in NASCAR Cup Series competition. Logano won his first race in New Hampshire at 19 years, 1 month, and 4 days old.

RICHMOND GRIDDLE POPCORN BAR

DIFFICULTY: Rookie | **PREP TIME:** 2 Minutes | **COOK TIME:** 6 Minutes | **SERVINGS:** 8 | **DIETARY:** V

RICHMOND RACEWAY BEGAN HOSTING just one NASCAR weekend during the season beginning in 2025, making it a must-see attraction and a coveted ticket. At this short track in Virginia, it's not uncommon to see sparks fly as drivers race in tight quarters, which can often lead to contact. It's how the track earned the nickname "the Action Track," because you can't look away! Enjoy the show with an equally exciting and super-delicious selection of toppings on griddled popcorn.

Popcorn oil, for popping

1 cup popcorn

Salt

TOPPINGS

Gummy bears

M&M's

Mini marshmallows

Caramel drizzle

Rainbow sprinkles

Mini chocolate chips

Chocolate coated raisins

Coconut flakes

Cinnamon

EQUIPMENT

Basting dome

1. Prepare the griddle for direct, medium heat cooking (350° to 400° F).
2. Place a generous amount of oil on the griddle followed by ½ cup of popcorn kernels.
3. Cover the popcorn with the basting dome and slide around the griddle frequently as the oil and popcorn begins to cook.
4. After several minutes, the popcorn will start to pop. Continue to move the dome around the griddle until the popping slows and to a single pop every few seconds, about 6 minutes total.
5. Remove the basting dome and transfer the popcorn to a serving bowl. Salt to taste.
6. Serve the popcorn with the toppings.

DRINKS

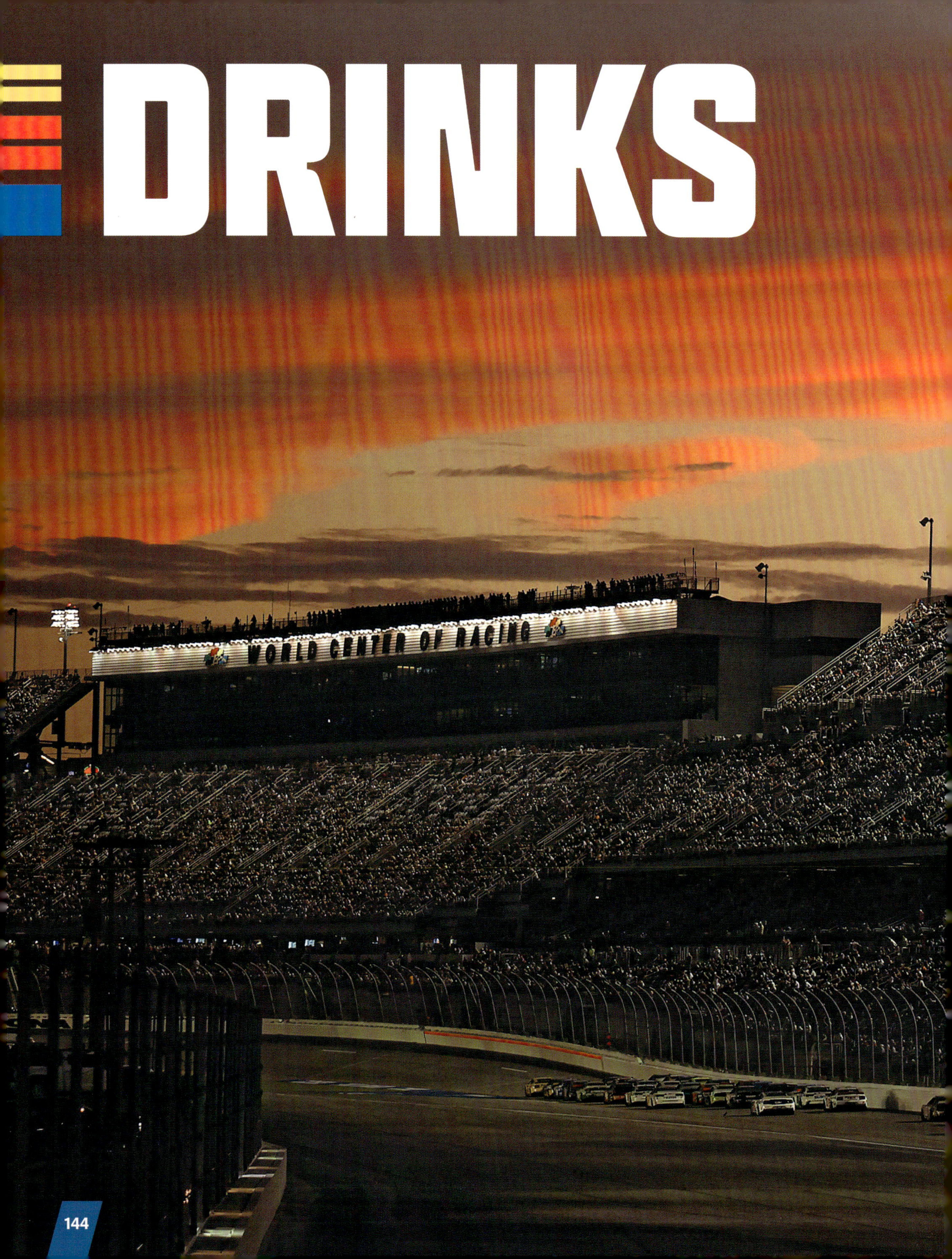

SafetyCulture
TRUEWERK

SPLASH & GO SHANDY

DIFFICULTY: Rookie | **PREP TIME:** 2 Minutes | **SERVINGS:** 2 | **DIETARY:** GF, V

RACE DAY ISN'T COMPLETE without a cold one to accompany good eats. If you're a NASCAR fan at a tailgate, then beer isn't hard to find. After all, Busch Beer is the official beer sponsor of NASCAR as well as Ross Chastain's No. 1 Trackhouse Racing Chevrolet. Don't be afraid to mix things up, though. In this case, mix that beer with the sweet, tart, refreshing taste of lemonade.

One 12-ounce bottle sparkling lemonade

One 12-ounce bottle lager beer

Sliced lemon, for serving

1. Divide the lemonade between two glasses. Top each with the beer, making a 50/50 ratio.
2. Stir and serve with lemon to garnish.

FUN FACT

Ross Chastain made a splash at the Martinsville Speedway in 2022 when he made a video game move by riding full throttle against the wall to gain positions. It was as exciting as it was unexpected. NASCAR has since outlawed the move in the name of safety.

DAYTONA BOURBON SMASH

DIFFICULTY: Rookie | **PREP TIME:** 2 Minutes | **SERVINGS:** 1 | **DIETARY:** GF, V

DAYTONA INTERNATIONAL SPEEDWAY IS the home of the Daytona 500, the biggest race on the NASCAR schedule. A world-class facility, Daytona provides incredible hospitality for race fans—from infield access that puts you on the other side of a garage window from your favorite driver to the unlimited amenities in the grandstands. Consider this Daytona Bourbon Smash the best of the cocktail world. You must include cups of its fresh, minty coolness at your next tailgate party.

1. In a shaker glass, muddle the lemon wedges, simple syrup, and several mint leaves.
2. Add the bourbon and fill with ice.
3. Shake vigorously for 15 seconds.
4. Add crushed ice to a rocks glass, then pour the cocktail into the rocks glass through a fine-mesh strainer.
5. Garnish with mint.

2 lemon wedges

¾ ounce simple syrup

2 mint sprigs

2 ounces bourbon

THE COOLER MANHATTAN

DIFFICULTY: Champion | **PREP TIME:** 6 Minutes | **SERVINGS:** 5 | **DIETARY:** V

WHEN YOU WANT THE fulfillment of a traditional Manhattan cocktail but with a modern twist and taste, reach for the Cooler Manhattan. It's like NASCAR deciding in 2022 that they would change things up by requiring the number on the race car to move farther forward, going from what had been the traditional location at the center of the door to behind the front tire. Both this slightly sweet drink and car number placement are different than expected but just as good. Unlike a traditional Manhattan cocktail, the cooler version, where it's meant to be held, is pre-mixed, giving you more time to watch the race and less time to tend the bar. Pour it up. Cheers!

One 750-milliliter bottle rye whiskey

5½ ounces sweet vermouth

23 dashes Angostura bitters

5½ ounces water

1. Remove 11 ounces of whiskey from the bottle and save for another use.
2. Using a funnel, add the vermouth, bitters, and water to the bottle.
3. Seal and invert the bottle several times to mix. Store in the freezer or a cooler until ready to serve. It's best if consumed in one month.

FUN FACT

A race car in NASCAR can also be described as a NASCAR "stock car," and the events are known as "stock car racing."

HOMESTEAD-MIAMI MEZCAL MARGARITA

DIFFICULTY: Champion | **PREP TIME:** 2 Minutes | **SMOKED ICE PREP:** 24 Hours | **SERVINGS:** 1 | **DIETARY:** GF, V

A TRIP TO THE Florida sun to visit the Homestead-Miami Speedway is always a refreshing treat because of its location and fantastic side-by-side racing. The best drivers at this oval track with its steep banking are the ones who can drive inches off the wall, which is the fastest way to make a lap time. This smoky, earthy cocktail is just as thrilling. If you want to impress with your tailgating skills, like the drivers impress on the track with theirs, be sure to use the smoked ice.

Lime, quartered, for the rim

Kosher salt

2 ounces mezcal

1 ounce Cointreau

1 ounce freshly squeezed lime juice

1 barspoon agave nectar

2 cups smoked ice (optional)

1. Rub a quartered lime around the rim of a cocktail glass. Put the salt on a small plate, then invert the glass and salt the rim.
2. To a cocktail shaker, combine the mezcal, Cointreau, lime juice, and agave.
3. Fill the cocktail shaker with smoked ice and shake vigorously for at least 15 seconds.
4. Strain into rocks glass. Garnish with the remaining lime wedges.

Smoked Ice

1. Pour 4 cups of water into a disposable foil pan.
2. Prepare the grill for indirect, low heat cooking (250° to 300° F).
3. If using a charcoal grill, add three or four wood chunks directly to the lit coals once the coals have ashed over. If using a gas grill, add the wood chunks to a pouch made of aluminum foil with holes poked through the top. Put the pouch directly over a lit burner. Once the gas or charcoal grill begins to release white, wispy smoke, it's ready.
4. Smoke the water over indirect low heat for 2 hours, stirring occasionally.
5. Remove from the grill and allow to cool. Pour into ice cube trays and freeze until ready to use.

GRILLED PINEAPPLE VODKA

DIFFICULTY: Rookie | **PREP TIME:** 2 Minutes | **COOK TIME:** 5 Hours | **SERVINGS:** 1 | **DIETARY:** GF, V

NOTHING BEATS BEING ABLE to attend a race with friends, and enjoying great good and wonderful beverages. Take a moment to toast to NASCAR race day—and a successful tailgate—with a glass of this divine, Grilled Pineapple Vodka. When you're craving a sweet beverage and want something that goes down smooth, look no further. This blend of pineapple and orange juice, and the addition of vodka, ice, and pineapple ring garnish, is the best way to wrap up a tailgate. Cheers!

1 canned pineapple ring
3 ounces orange juice
3 ounces pineapple juice
2 ounces vodka

1. Prepare the grill for direct, medium heat cooking (350° to 400° F).
2. Grill the pineapple ring over direct heat until marked, 4 to 5 minutes, flipping once. Remove.
3. In a cocktail shaker filled with ice, add the juices, vodka, and ice. Shake vigorously for 15 seconds.
4. Fill a large glass with ice and strain the cocktail into the glass. Garnish with the pineapple ring and serve.

FUN FACT

NASCAR is the most watched and popular motorsport in the United States. At the racetrack, each venue offers unique camping and tailgating experiences for race fans to enjoy the sport.

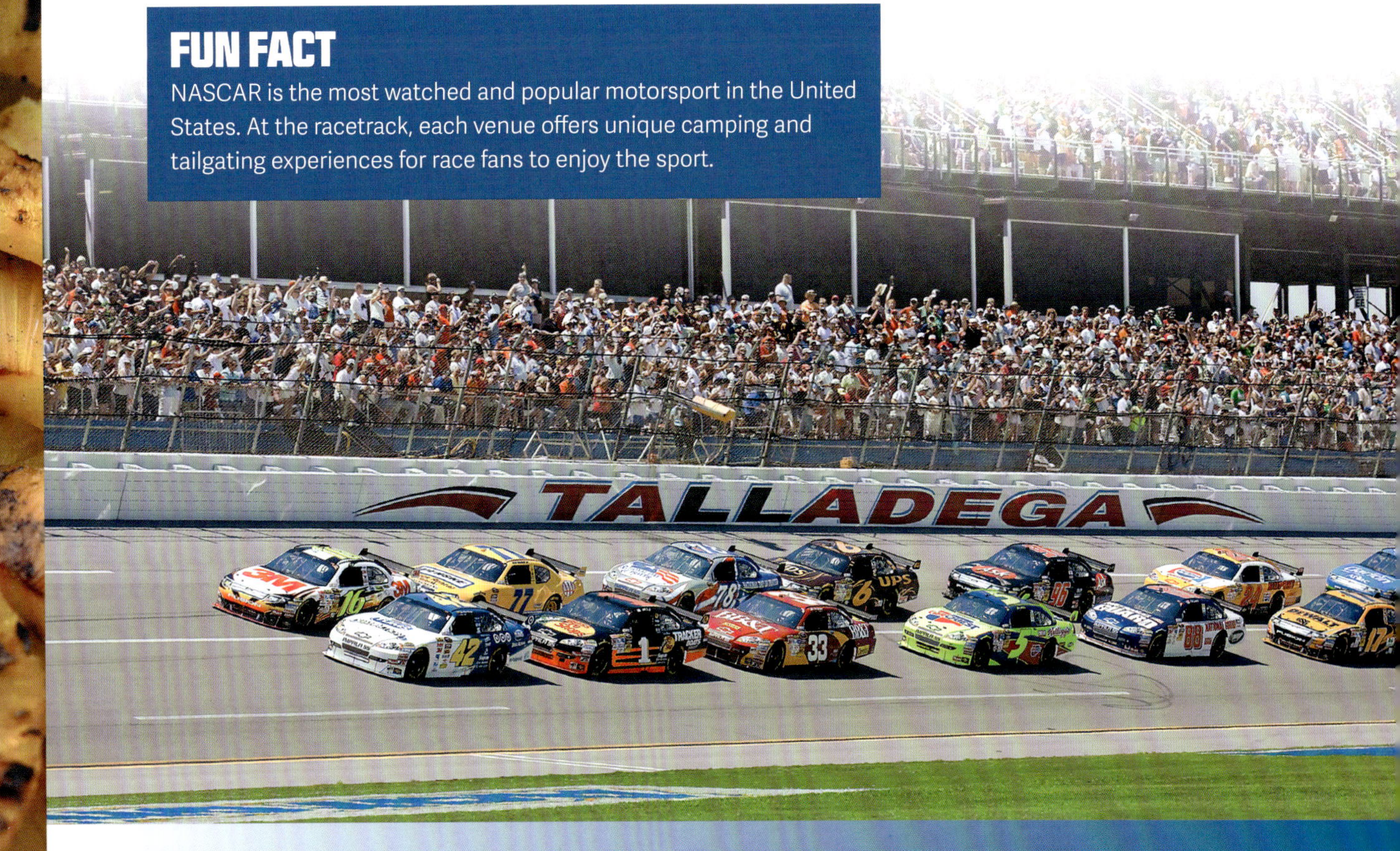

DIFFICULTY INDEX

Rookie

Champion

Veteran

CONVERSION CHARTS

VOLUME

US	METRIC
⅕ teaspoon (tsp)	1 ml
1 teaspoon (tsp)	5 ml
1 tablespoon	15 ml
1 fluid ounce	30 ml
⅕ cup	50 ml
¼ cup	60 ml
⅓ cup	80 ml
3.4 fluid ounces	100 ml
½ cup	120 ml
⅔ cup	160 ml
¾ cup	180 ml
1 cup	240 ml
1 pint (2 cups)	480 ml
1 quart (4 cups)	.95 liter

WEIGHT

US	METRIC
0.5 ounce (oz)	14 grams
1 ounce (oz)	28 grams
¼ pound (lbs)	113 grams
⅓ pound (lbs)	151 grams
½ pound (lbs)	227 grams
1 pound (lbs)	454 grams

TEMPERATURES

FAHRENHEIT	CELSIUS
200°	93°
212°	100°
250°	120°
275°	135°
300°	150°
325°	165°
350°	177°
400°	205°
425°	220°
450°	233°
475°	245°
500°	260°

ABOUT THE AUTHORS

JOEY LOGANO is a three-time NASCAR Cup Series Champion. Driving No. 22 Team Penske Ford Mustang, Logano is the only active driver with three Cup Series championships on his resume. The 2015 Daytona 500 winner has thirty-six career NCS victories, which ranks twenty-sixth on the series' all-time wins list. Logano's 2024 Cup Series title placed him among the sport's greats, becoming one of ten drivers of all time with three or more championships and one of four drivers to win three titles before the age of thirty-five, joining Richard Petty, Jeff Gordon, and Jimmie Johnson. Away from the racetrack, Logano and his wife, Brittany, were honored with the 2018 Comcast Community Champion of the Year award for their charitable efforts with the Joey Logano Foundation. Logano and Brittany have two young sons, Hudson and Jameson, and a daughter, Emilia.

MIKE LANG is the stomach behind the long-running food and beer blog *Another Pint Please* and the author of the cookbook *One-Beer Grilling*. He is happiest behind the camera and at the grill, where his work is seen worldwide as the "Grillographer" for Weber Grills. Most days, Mike can be found working in his grilling studio, surrounded by over fifty grills, each ready for their next meal. Mike recently retired as a decorated police sergeant after serving thirty-two distinguished years with the Englewood Police Department in southwest Ohio.

KELLY CRANDALL has been on the NASCAR beat full-time since 2013 and has been the chief NASCAR writer for Racer.com since 2017. Her work has also appeared on NASCAR.com, in USA Today, and on NBC Sports. She is a regular contributor to SiriusXM NASCAR Radio (Channel 90) and a NASCAR feature writer for ESPN. A corporate communications graduate from Central Penn College, Crandall is a two-time George Cunningham Writer of the Year recipient from the National Motorsports Press Association.

PO Box 3088
San Rafael, CA 94912
www.insighteditions.com
Find us on Facebook: www.facebook.com/InsightEditions
Follow us on Instagram: @insighteditions

Published by Insight Editions, San Rafael, California, in 2025.

ISBN: 979-8-3374-0064-8

Publisher: Raoul Goff
SVP, Group Publisher: Vanessa Lopez
VP, Creative: Chrissy Kwasnik
VP, Manufacturing: Alix Nicholaeff
Publishing Director: Mike Degler
Art Director: Catherine San Juan
Junior Designer: Samuel Louie
Executive Editor: Jennifer Sims
Senior Editor: Eric Geron
Editorial Assistants: Jeff Chiarelli, Alecsander Zapata
Managing Editor: Nora Milman
Production Manager: Deena Hashem
Strategic Production Planner: Lina s Palma-Temena

ROOTS of PEACE REPLANTED PAPER

Insight Editions, in association with Roots of Peace, will plant two trees for each tree used in the manufacturing of this book. Roots of Peace is an internationally renowned humanitarian organization dedicated to eradicating land mines worldwide and converting war-torn lands into productive farms and wildlife habitats. Roots of Peace will plant two million fruit and nut trees in Afghanistan and provide farmers there with the skills and support necessary for sustainable land use.

Manufactured in China by Insight Editions

10 9 8 7 6 5 4 3 2 1